The Open University

D0531269

Investigating Intelligence

Jovan Byford, Jean McAvoy and Philip Banyard

This publication forms part of the Open University module DE100 Investigating psychology 1. Details of this and other Open University modules can be obtained from the Student Registration and Enquiry Service, The Open University, PO Box 197, Milton Keynes MK7 6BJ, United Kingdom (tel. +44 (0)845 300 60 90; email general-enquiries@open.ac.uk).

Alternatively, you may visit the Open University website at www.open.ac.uk where you can learn more about the wide range of modules and packs offered at all levels by The Open University.

To purchase a selection of Open University materials visit www.ouw.co.uk, or contact Open University Worldwide, Walton Hall, Milton Keynes MK7 6AA, United Kingdom for a catalogue (tel. +44 (0)1908 858779; fax +44 (0)1908 858787; email ouw-customer-services@open.ac.uk).

The Open University, Walton Hall, Milton Keynes MK7 6AA

First published 2014

Edited and designed by The Open University.

Printed and bound in the United Kingdom by Halstan & Co. Ltd, Amersham, Bucks.

ISBN 978 1 7800 7960 8

1.1

Contents

Introduction

Welcome to *Investigating Intelligence*. This is the first book you will read as part of your study of DE100 *Investigating psychology 1*. As the title of the book suggests, the main topic is intelligence, a concept that you are likely to have come across even if you have never studied psychology. Most of us have at least a rough idea of what we mean by intelligence. In everyday language, the word 'intelligence' is commonly used to describe the kind of qualities and abilities we associate with being 'smart' or 'clever'.

Although, for centuries, people have been interested in the question of what it means to be 'intelligent' and what makes some people smarter than others, it is only since the mid nineteenth century that these questions have been the topic of scientific enquiry. Psychology has played a central role in this development, and intelligence remains one of the key areas of interest to psychologists. However, as you will see, intelligence is also one of the most controversial topics in psychology.

Over the coming weeks, you will have the opportunity to engage with the story of psychological research on intelligence and specifically on intelligence measurement. As will become apparent, one of the central assumptions about human intelligence, and a major preoccupation for psychologists interested in the topic, has been that it can be measured. This focus on measurement has shaped much of the way in which intelligence research has developed. You will learn about the origins of modern-day intelligence tests, about different explanations for why some people are considered to be more intelligent than others, and about some of the current debates about intelligence and its usefulness both in psychology and in applied settings.

What makes intelligence a fascinating area of psychological research, and a useful starting point in the study of psychology, is that it occupies a somewhat curious status within the discipline. In some quarters, intelligence, and particularly the measurement of intelligence, is seen as one of psychology's greatest success stories (Deary, 2001; Nisbett et al., 2012). This view is reinforced by the fact that intelligence testing is today commonly used in educational selection, in certain areas of job recruitment, in diagnosing learning disability, in clinical assessment and in other professional and practical settings. Underpinning this use of intelligence testing is the widespread belief that performance on these tests predicts things such as academic and professional success, or ability to cope with everyday tasks (Asbury and Plomin, 2013). In fact, intelligence testing is today so pervasive that it is quite likely that most people growing up in the Western world will at some point in their life encounter an intelligence test, in one form or another.

Surprisingly, perhaps, this confidence in intelligence testing persists alongside a broader realisation that this is also one of the most disputed topics in psychology. While some psychologists promote intelligence measurement, others have dismissed it as a 'failed idea' (Murdoch, 2007). Many psychologists have questioned whether a singular concept such as 'intelligence' can usefully capture the diversity of human skills and abilities. What is more, as you will find out in the chapters that follow, intelligence research has a pronounced *political* dimension. Historically, the seemingly obvious finding that people differ in ability has all too often been interpreted as implying that some people, and more importantly some sections of society, are inherently more or less intelligent, or intellectually able, than others. As Leon Kamin, an outspoken critic of intelligence testing, put it, psychological research on intelligence has traditionally served as little more than 'an instrument of oppression against the poor – dressed up in the trappings of science, rather than politics' (Kamin, 1974, p. 1).

Thus, the history of intelligence research has been one of continuous debate, polarisation of opinion, and dispute. *Investigating Intelligence* presents a short introduction to some of the issues that have defined these debates. Furthermore, in the process of exploring the history and development of psychological research on human intelligence, this book introduces some of the core themes that run throughout DE100 *Investigating psychology 1*. These broader themes include how knowledge about mind and behaviour evolves over time, through scientific research, but also through discussion and debate about the merits of that research; the ways in which topics in psychology emerge from a need to solve both intellectual and practical problems; and how broader historical and social events influence the way in which psychological research is conducted and applied. Perhaps most importantly, some of the weaknesses of intelligence research offer a powerful reminder of why it is necessary to always critically engage with research findings. As you will be reminded throughout your study of psychology, learning about the human – and non-human – mind and behaviour, and indeed being a psychologist, involves questioning and evaluating the way that scientific evidence has been collected and interpreted, and scrutinising the conclusions that have been drawn from it. Nowhere is this need for critical engagement with evidence more apparent than in some of the early research on human intelligence.

Next, we will consider the question of what intelligence actually is. As you will see, researchers have found it surprisingly difficult to pin down the precise meaning of this term.

What is intelligence?

When introducing a new concept, most textbooks will start by providing a definition. The purpose of a definition is to capture, usually in a sentence or two, the essence of whatever it is that is being introduced, an agreed meaning of a term. This is indeed the practice that you will encounter throughout your study of DE100. However, when it comes to intelligence, providing a definition is not that straightforward. Although psychologists, like most people, tend to have quite clear ideas about what sorts of things are characteristic of 'intelligence', they have not been able to agree on precisely what these are or, therefore, settle on a single definition.

Activity 1

Spend a couple of minutes thinking of the kind of abilities you consider to be associated with 'intelligence'. What sort of things can a supposedly 'intelligent person' do?

How did you find this task? Did you come up with examples such as 'solve problems', 'pick up the meaning of complex material', 'remember lots of information', 'learn quickly', 'think on one's feet'? These and many other characteristics are indeed the sort of things that, in everyday language, tend to be associated with being 'smart', 'clever' and 'intelligent'.

Now have a look at the following small selection of definitions which have been offered in psychological literature on intelligence over the past hundred or so years. Between them the definitions suggest a wide range of characteristics. See if you can identify a common set of characteristics around which you could begin to build a definition.

[Intelligence] is judgement, otherwise known as common sense, practical good sense, initiative, the ability to adapt oneself to circumstance. To judge well, to comprehend well, to reason well, these are the essential ingredients of intelligence.

(Binet and Simon [1905], cited in Mackintosh, 2011, p. 12)

We shall use the term 'intelligence' to mean the ability of an organism to solve new problems.

(Bingham, 1937, p. 36)

A global concept that involves an individual's ability to act purposefully, think rationally, and deal effectively with the environment.

(Wechsler, 1958, p. 7)

[Intelligence] involves the ability to reason, plan, solve problems, think abstractly, comprehend complex ideas, learn quickly and learn from experience. It is not merely book learning, a narrow academic skill ... Rather it reflects a broader and deeper capability for comprehending our surroundings – 'catching on', 'making sense' of things, or 'figuring out' what to do.

(Gottfredson, 1997, p. 13)

The first thing you may have noticed is that many different terms are employed to describe intelligence. There is talk of common sense, initiative, adaptability, reasoning, acting purposefully, problem solving, even planning. All of these are very different abilities, yet they are subsumed under the common category of 'intelligence'. Also, you may have noticed that Gottfredson's definition in particular resorts to rather vague terms, such as 'catching on', 'making sense', 'figuring out'. This is unusual for formal definitions, but reflects the inherent elusiveness of the concept of intelligence.

The problem with defining intelligence is not new; it has plagued research on the topic from its inception. In the early 1920s, at the time when intelligence tests were becoming increasingly promoted as an important aspect of psychological research and practice, the editors of the US-based *Journal of Educational Psychology* conducted a small survey among leading American experts on intelligence testing. The experts were asked to define what it was they were actually trying to measure. When the answers came in, it became clear that while all the respondents were convinced about the existence of something called 'intelligence', they could not agree on what it was. Some mentioned things like abstract thinking or distinguishing 'truth' from 'falsehood'; others referred to the ability to suppress one's instincts and act rationally, or the capacity to learn from experience, and so on (Sternberg, 2000). Some 60 years later, when Sternberg and Detterman (1986) asked the same question of a new generation of intelligence researchers, they obtained very similar results: researchers simply could not agree on the defining criteria of intelligence.

As you read through the chapters that follow, you will start to see why pinning down the meaning of intelligence has proved so challenging. This has to do with both the nature of the phenomenon, and how psychologists have sought to study it. Nevertheless, in spite of the variety of different definitions that have been proposed, much of intelligence research is based on three broad points of agreement. First, that a whole range of specific abilities that enable a person to function effectively in their environment (including things featured in the definitions above, such as learning from experience, problem solving, making sense of things, etc.) are *underpinned by a broader ability called 'intelligence'*. Second, that intelligence *varies between people*, in that it is inevitable that some people will be more intellectually able than others. The third point of agreement is that intelligence is *important*, because it accounts for how well a person will perform at school or in the workplace, or deal with intellectual challenges in life. Throughout this book we will explore, and critically examine, all three of these claims about human intelligence.

Chapter outline

Investigating Intelligence consists of three chapters. The opening chapter, 'Measuring intelligence', introduces the history of intelligence testing and some of the challenges faced by those who have sought to measure human intellectual abilities. You will learn about the pioneering work of the Frenchman Alfred Binet, who in the early twentieth century developed the first modern intelligence test. Binet's work proved highly influential and some of the principles of intelligence measurement which he established are still apparent in tests used today. You will also learn about the basic features of a contemporary intelligence test – the Wechsler Adult Intelligence Scale. More importantly, in this first chapter, you will begin to engage with the issue of what it is that intelligence tests actually measure. Do they assess some basic mental ability that differentiates the inherently clever from those that are not, as advocates of intelligence testing suggest? Or is performance on tests influenced by things like a person's social or cultural background, their drive, motivation, confidence and experience, and therefore by things that have little to do with intrinsic ability as such?

Chapter 2, 'Explaining differences in intelligence', continues with this theme by exploring some of the explanations that have been proposed for why people differ in intelligence. At the core of the question is the contentious issue of whether some people are simply born clever, or whether differences in intelligence are due to environmental factors such as differences in experience, educational opportunities or social status. You will read about some of the controversial attempts to explain differences in intelligence in terms of biological inheritance, but also about the alternative proposition, that understanding individual differences in intelligence requires us to pay closer attention to a more complex set of influences, including class and cultural background.

The final chapter, Chapter 3, 'Beyond the IQ', goes beyond the established approaches to intelligence testing to consider three specific, and related, issues relevant to current studies of intelligence. First, it looks at the possibility of creating a measure of intelligence that is independent of culturally specific knowledge and experience. This is an issue that cuts to the heart of what intelligence actually is, and whether there is such a thing as 'pure' intellectual, or reasoning, ability. Second, the chapter explores how intelligence measurement is used to determine whether or not a person has a learning disability. It examines the merits of this long-standing practice, and considers some alternative ways of thinking about learning disability and how it should be diagnosed. Finally, the chapter looks at the concept of *emotional intelligence*, and whether the ability to understand and manage emotion is a useful alternative to the traditional way of thinking about the kind of skills and abilities that help make us competent actors in our everyday lives.

As you read through the chapters, it is likely that you will encounter some terms with which you are not yet familiar, or terms whose meaning in psychology is different from their everyday use. Don't be alarmed by this. All the technical terms will be introduced as you go along, both within the text and as marginal definitions. There is also an online glossary on the module website which contains the definitions of terms featured not just in this book, but in all three DE100 module texts. Most important of all, you will encounter many of these concepts again over the course of your study, so there will be further opportunities to develop and consolidate your understanding.

Finally, it is worth pointing out that engaging with the topic of intelligence can be challenging in different ways. It may have personal resonance for those who have been exposed to intelligence tests in the past, whether at school, in the workplace or in another setting, especially if that experience has not been positive. Reading about intelligence may also pose challenges to those for whom intelligence forms an important part of their self-understanding: some people might think of themselves as particularly intelligent, while others, for one reason or another, might view themselves as lacking in particular intellectual abilities. Reading about the history of intelligence research may raise questions about those self-understandings. Whatever your personal opinion about intelligence and intelligence testing may be, the important thing is that you approach the arguments presented in this book with an open mind. Psychological research has revealed human intelligence to be a lot more complex than is generally presumed, and it is likely that as you read the chapters you will begin to question your own assumptions about what it means to be 'intelligent'. Crucially, we cannot promise definitive answers or solutions to the questions that may arise, but hopefully your exploration of human intelligence will make you aware of the intricacy of the human mind, and whet your appetite for the study of psychology.

Jovan Byford, Jean McAvoy and Philip Banyard

References

Asbury, K. and Plomin, R. (2013) *G is for Genes: The Impact of Genetics on Education and Achievement*, Chichester, John Wiley & Sons.

Bingham, W. V. (1937) *Aptitudes and Aptitude Testing*, New York, NY, Harper & Brothers.

Deary, I. J. (2001) *Intelligence: A Very Short Introduction*, Oxford, Oxford University Press.

Gottfredson, L. S. (1997) 'Mainstream science on intelligence: an editorial with 52 signatories, history, and bibliography', *Intelligence*, vol. 24, pp. 13–23.

Kamin, L. (1974) *The Science and Politics of IQ*, Harmondsworth, Penguin.

Mackintosh, N. J. (2011) *IQ and Human Intelligence*, Oxford, Oxford University Press.

Murdoch, S. (2007) *IQ: A Smart History of a Failed Idea*, Hoboken, NJ, John Wiley & Sons.

Nisbett, R. E., Aronson, J., Blair, C., Dickens, W., Flynn, J., Halpern, D. F. and Turkheimer, E. (2012) 'Intelligence: new findings and theoretical developments', *American Psychologist*, vol. 67, no. 2, pp. 130–59.

Sternberg, R. J. (2000) 'The concept of intelligence', in Sternberg, R. J. (ed.) *The Handbook of Intelligence*, Cambridge, Cambridge University Press.

Sternberg, R. J. and Detterman, D. K. (eds) (1986) *What Is Intelligence? Contemporary Viewpoints on Its Nature and Definition*, Norwood, NJ, Ablex.

Wechsler, D. (1958) *The Measurement and Appraisal of Adult Intelligence*, 4th edn, Baltimore, MD, The Williams & Wilkins Company.

Chapter 1
Measuring intelligence

Contents

Aims and objectives

After studying this chapter you should be able to:

- describe Alfred Binet's early attempt to measure intelligence
- identify some of the main features of an intelligence test, and the principles behind test design
- outline what IQ is, and discuss the assumption of normal distribution of intelligence
- appreciate the complex nature of intelligence and the challenges posed by attempting to measure aspects of human psychology that cannot be directly observed.

1 Introduction

Every year, thousands of children in the UK sit school entrance examinations, previously known as the 11-plus exam, in the hope of obtaining a place in one of the couple of hundred remaining grammar schools. This exam, which was once compulsory in all state-funded schools, serves as an instrument of academic selection: performance on a series of tests is used to determine children's educational choices, and opportunities.

Figure 1.1   School test at age 11: an instrument of academic selection

The precursor to the 11-plus was introduced in 1944 as part of a wider educational reform. At that time the exam was compulsory, and its aim was to establish what kind of school a child was best suited to: a grammar school, a secondary modern school or one of the technical schools. The different schools were designed to prepare students for different career paths and therefore had a major influence on the children's future. In practice, the test functioned, just like today's entrance examinations, as a way of determining who was considered 'clever enough' to attend one of the highly regarded grammar schools.

From its inception, the 11-plus was based on two assumptions. First, that a person's intellectual ability can be measured with some accuracy at a fairly early age, and therefore, that selection can be meaningfully carried out before the start of secondary school. Second, that this selection should not be made on the basis of the child's knowledge acquired in school up to that point, or things such as individual motivation or social skills. Rather, the child was to be assessed on a set of more general reasoning and problem-solving abilities.

These assumptions mirror much of the psychological research on intelligence testing. This is not a coincidence. Research on intelligence has helped inform educational policy since the early twentieth century, including the development of the 11-plus exam. In fact, the 11-plus *is* a form of intelligence test in regard to the kind of questions it asks and abilities it assesses.

In this chapter, we will look more closely at the idea that the differences between people in terms of their reasoning skills, the ability to think abstractly, solve problems, apprehend relations between things in the world, etc., can be measured. This is an important issue in the light of the point raised in the Introduction, namely, that there is considerable disagreement among researchers about what intelligence actually is. So, how does one go about measuring, and studying, an elusive and intangible concept such as intelligence? What is it that intelligence tests measure, and how?

We will begin to explore these questions by considering the history of intelligence measurement, specifically the emergence of the first modern intelligence test.

Summary

- Grammar school entrance examinations, which used to be known as the 11-plus exam, are based on tests of intelligence.
- Both intelligence tests and entrance exams such as the 11-plus rely on the assumption that a person's intellectual ability can be meaningfully measured at an early age, and that this can be done through a set of more general reasoning and problem-solving tasks.

2   The first test of intelligence

The fundamental notion behind the idea of intelligence is that people differ in their mental abilities. This is neither a new nor a particularly remarkable proposition. Ancient Greek philosophers, for example, were well aware that the ability to think abstractly varies across the population and they debated extensively whether this ability is **innate** or the outcome of learning. In the Middle Ages, the term 'intelligence' was used to describe what differentiates 'dull' and 'bright' students, while in later centuries philosophers and writers speculated widely on different 'types' of human intelligence and their origins (Richardson, 1998).

However, it was only in the late nineteenth century, with the emergence of psychology as a scientific discipline, that intelligence became the object of systematic research. A prominent role in this development was played by a Frenchman, Alfred Binet, whose pioneering work in assessing children's developmental levels we will consider next.

Innate
Relating to a behaviour, ability, disposition or characteristic that is present from birth rather than being acquired through experience.

2.1   Alfred Binet: from measuring heads to measuring ability

In the second half of the nineteenth century, much of intelligence research focused on **craniometry** – the measurement of people's heads (Gould, 1996). The assumption was that there is a direct relationship between head *size* and intelligence, in the sense that a big head carries a big brain, and this would correspond with high intelligence. There were also those, like Sir Francis Galton in England, who believed that intelligence can be assessed not only by measuring the size of a person's skull, but also by looking at performance on a range of simple *physical* tasks, such as tests of eyesight, strength of grip, colour vision, hearing, hand preference, and so on. In 1884, Galton created a mental testing laboratory in the South Kensington Museum in London (today's Science Museum), where he charged visitors for the privilege of having their intelligence tested in his 'anthropometric laboratory' – the laboratory for measuring humans (Murdoch, 2007). Galton's approach to intelligence measurement followed the basic principle of craniometry, namely that some higher order 'natural ability' underpins both a person's physical properties and their mental aptitude, and therefore by measuring head size, or performance on physical tasks, one can draw conclusions about intelligence.

Craniometry
The study of people's intellectual abilities based on the shape and size of their head. In Chapter 7 of *Investigating Psychology* you will read more about how, in the nineteenth century, the size and shape of people's heads were used to draw conclusions not only about their abilities, but also about their personality.

Figure 1.2   Galton's anthropometric laboratory, 1884

Meanwhile, in France a young scientist, Alfred Binet (1857–1911), was developing a different approach. Although Binet initially studied law, he never pursued a career as a lawyer. Instead, he became interested in medical science. He gained employment at the Salpêtrière Hospital in Paris, where he worked with Jean-Martin Charcot, the person often regarded as the founder of modern **neurology** – the scientific study of the brain and the nervous system. At Salpêtrière, Binet worked on topics as diverse as child development, visual illusions, mental illness and hypnotism. Later, in 1891, he moved to the then recently created psychology laboratory at Paris's most prestigious university, the Sorbonne, where he remained until his death in 1911.

At his laboratory at the Sorbonne, Binet had spent many years studying the relationship between intelligence and head size in schoolchildren. Eventually, he became disillusioned with craniometry as a method for measuring intelligence. Binet found that in most instances differences in head size were too small (often just a few millimetres) to account for the considerable variation in children's intellectual ability. More importantly, the differences were not consistent, so children who performed poorly in school often had bigger heads than the children

Neurology
The scientific study of the brain and the nervous system.

Figure 1.3   Alfred Binet (1857–1911)

who performed well. This meant that head size was a poor predictor of mental ability, and was, as such, useless for assessing the intelligence of individual children (Gould, 1996). Also, Binet became a fierce critic of craniometry as a supposedly 'objective' method of studying human psychology. Reflecting on his own work and that of his colleagues, Binet pointed to a phenomenon that has since become known as **confirmatory bias** (Rosenthal, 1966). He realised that, sometimes, scientists' expectations can unconsciously influence the outcome of their research. Specifically, Binet noticed that because craniometrists *expected* to find a difference between the head size, shape and volume of high and low achievers, they tended to, 'unconsciously and in good faith', measure heads in such a way as to confirm their expectations (Binet, cited in Gould, 1996, p. 177). This means that they tended to find that supposedly 'intelligent heads' are larger or more voluminous than the 'unintelligent' ones, even though, in reality, there was no difference between them.

Confirmatory bias
When a scientist's expectations unconsciously influence the outcome of their research. This occurs because of the tendency to pay most attention to those features of a phenomenon that appear to confirm prior expectations.

Psychometrics
A field of study in psychology concerned with psychological measurement of things like attitudes, personality traits, mood or intelligence.

Personality
A person's stable and enduring traits and characteristics (e.g. whether they are outgoing, assertive, perceptive or emotional) which lead them to behave in a steady way over time. You will learn more about personality and how it is measured in Chapter 1 of *Investigating Psychology*.

Individual differences
Any characteristics that are susceptible to variation between individuals; for example, personality or intelligence.

Battery of tests
A series of tests aimed at measuring the same thing, such as intelligence.

The disappointment with craniometry led Binet to abandon this method and move to the kind of testing which has been associated with intelligence measurement ever since, namely **psychometrics**. Psychometrics is the field of psychology devoted to psychological measurement and the construction of questionnaires and tests which can be used to assess things like knowledge, attitudes, mood, **personality** traits, or mental ability. Because psychometrics focuses on how individuals *differ* from each other in ability, performance, disposition or behaviour, it is closely related to the area of psychology known as the psychology of **individual differences**.

2.2 The Binet–Simon test

In 1895, Binet began work on a **battery of tests** designed to measure individual differences in intelligence, or what he referred to as 'higher mental power'. Success came a decade later, after he started collaboration with a young doctor, Théodore Simon. In France at that time the government had just introduced a policy of basic education for all children. Problems emerged with children who could not keep up with the curriculum and, in particular, with some children whose performance in school was so weak that it was questioned whether they would benefit from education at all. In 1904, the French government set up a commission that included both Simon and Binet, and asked it to devise a reliable way of identifying children with special educational needs. The following year, the Binet–Simon test, which was to bring its authors international fame, was published for the first time (Murdoch, 2007). Binet continued to refine the measure, and the final version of the Binet–Simon test was completed shortly before his death in 1911.

The primary purpose of the Binet–Simon test was to help identify children who, in terms of their intellectual development, lagged behind their peers. As part of the test, children were asked to perform a series of short tasks, such as following commands, naming objects in pictures, defining abstract words, memorising spoken numbers, comparing lines of unequal length, and so on (see Table 1.1 for examples). There were 54 tasks in total and they were arranged in order of difficulty. When assessing a child, the person administering the test would start with the simplest questions, those that even the youngest children sitting the test (3-year-olds) would be expected to answer correctly. As the test progressed, the questions would get harder, and the testing would continue until the child could no longer manage the complexity. Usually the test took around 40 minutes to complete. In the end, the child's overall performance on the different tasks was compared to what was considered to be the norm for different age groups, in order to establish their relative 'intellectual level' or 'mental age'. For example, if a child's performance was comparable to that expected of a child aged 4 (they could perform tasks expected of a 4-year-old, but not those expected of a 5-year-old), they would be said to have the mental age of 4. If the child in question was 3 years old (their 'chronological age' was 3), this result would be taken as evidence that they were quite advanced for their age. However, for a 5-year-old, the same result on the test would indicate a developmental delay of one year (Richardson, 1998).

Table 1.1   Examples of the tasks used in the Binet–Simon test for children aged 3–7. The test went up to the age of 16, which was considered to be the adult level of intelligence

	Average child of this age should be able to
Age 3	• Point to nose, eyes and mouth • Repeat two digits • List objects in a picture • Give their surname • Repeat a sentence of six syllables
Age 4	• Say if they are a boy or a girl • Name a key, a knife and a penny • Repeat three digits • Compare the length of two lines
Age 5	• Compare two weights • Copy a square • Repeat a sentence of ten syllables • Count four pennies • Put together the halves of a divided rectangle
Age 6	• Distinguish between morning and afternoon • Define a familiar word • Copy a picture of a diamond • Count 13 pennies • Distinguish pictures of ugly and pretty faces

Age 7	•	Identify right and left ear
	•	Describe a picture
	•	Execute three commands given simultaneously
	•	Count the value of six coins, comprised of three penny coins and three two-penny pieces
	•	Name four prime colours

(Source: adapted from Aiken and Groth-Marnat, 2006, p. 113)

In 1908, the Binet–Simon test was translated into English by the American psychologist Henry Goddard. In 1916, it was amended by Goddard's colleague Lewis Terman, who named his version the Stanford–Binet test, after Stanford University in California where Terman was professor of psychology. Goddard and Terman popularised the test in the United States and internationally, and the Stanford–Binet soon became regarded as the gold standard of intelligence testing (Murdoch, 2007). In the century since then, researchers continued to revise and refine the test, and a new version is still published every 20 years or so. The most recent, fifth version of the Stanford–Binet test (the SB-V) was published in 2003 (Aiken and Groth-Marnat, 2006).

2.3   The legacy of Alfred Binet

Binet's innovative work on intelligence left an important legacy. It resulted in the first modern test of intelligence. Also, in terms of both form and content, it served as a blueprint for subsequent tests.

Activity 1.1

Table 1.1 contains some examples of questions from the Binet–Simon test. Have a closer look at the items and see if you can make a list of the kind of abilities that the test assesses or measures. Which item strikes you as the oddest for an intelligence test?

The first thing to note is that the different items in the test appear to assess different abilities. Items that involve repeating digits or sentences can be seen as tests of *short-term memory*. Some items clearly require *verbal* ability, and good command of language: naming objects, defining familiar words, describing a picture. Other tasks, such as counting pennies, require numerical skills. There are also what might be called basic *general knowledge* questions such as naming colours, stating correctly one's gender, or distinguishing between morning and afternoon. Finally, there are questions that require drawing objects or solving puzzles involving shapes. These do not require knowledge of language or numbers, but a different kind of ability often referred to as *non-verbal reasoning*. In the Binet–Simon test, performance on these different kinds of tasks was used to derive an overall measure of intelligence. In fact, the specific abilities measured in Binet's test – short-term memory, verbal and numerical skills, non-verbal reasoning, general knowledge, and so on – feature in most subsequent intelligence tests. As you will see in Section 4, the Wechsler Adult Intelligence **Scale** (WAIS), probably the most widely used intelligence test in the world today, builds on many of the principles established by Binet. As far as the oddest item among the examples in Table 1.1 is concerned, it is probably the one about identifying ugly and pretty faces. This item seems to rely on judgement and taste rather than knowledge or intellectual ability. This is the kind of question that you will not find in intelligence tests today.

A further legacy of Binet's pioneering work is the notion that intelligence should be assessed only in relation to the population for which the test is intended. In children, this means that each child's performance on a test is only relevant when compared with the performance of other children. In adults, this implies that a measure of intelligence points not to some absolute standard of intellectual ability, but only to where a person's abilities are in relation to other adults, at that point in time. This has important implications for the development and application of intelligence tests. Before a test can be used in practice, benchmarks, or standards, for that test have to be established against which individual performance can be judged. For example, what ability can be expected of a child of a specific age? Or, what is the typical adult performance on the tasks measured by the test? In the case of the Binet–Simon test, the **test norms** which provided the basis for interpreting results were based on what research at the time indicated could be expected of a child of a certain age. These days, however, norms are usually developed using a different method known as **test standardisation**. This involves administering the test to a large sample of the population, with the view of obtaining a more reliable estimate of what a typical, or average, performance on a test would be for a particular age group, or population.

Scale
A term which, in the context of intelligence research, is often used instead of the word 'test'. In psychology, the word 'scale' refers to any set of questionnaire items or tasks which combine to measure a bigger construct that cannot be measured directly, such as intelligence or personality. You will learn about personality scales and how they are constructed in Chapter 1 of *Investigating Psychology*.

Test norms
Benchmarks used to assess an individual's performance on intelligence tests. They offer insight into how a person's test score compares with the scores of other test takers from the same population.

Test standardisation
The process of establishing test norms by administering the test to a large sample of the population for which the test is intended. We will return to the issue of standardisation and why it is important in Chapter 2 of *Investigating Intelligence*.

Finally, when evaluating Binet's contribution to psychology, it is important to note a feature of his work which sets him apart from his contemporaries, and indeed from many of those who in subsequent years continued to study intelligence. Binet's central motivation was to solve a practical problem: to find a simple, expedient and reliable tool that teachers could use to identify children with additional developmental or educational needs. He was a firm believer in the role of environment and education. He warned that even when children performed at two or three years below their chronological age, this did not mean that they had permanent learning disabilities, or that society should give up on their education. Intelligence, for Binet, was not a fixed thing. On the contrary, it was his view that disadvantaged children could be prepared for school, and their intelligence could be developed, with mental exercises. In the right environment, with the right support, intelligence could grow.

This approach to intelligence, which emphasises the importance of environment, stands in sharp contrast to the dominant trend at the time. Many of Binet's contemporaries, including Francis Galton and the craniometrists, treated intelligence as an inherited, innate and fixed property, a bit like the size and shape of the head. What is more, they used intelligence measurement not only to assess the abilities of individuals, but also to compare the intelligence of *groups*. They used their questionable methods to compare upper and lower classes, people of different racial backgrounds, men and women, and they routinely drew conclusions that reinforced the social inequalities and prejudices prevalent at the time. The claim that races, classes and genders differ in intelligence, in a way that always places the privileged groups on top and presents them as 'superior', was used to portray the existing social divisions and hierarchies as 'natural' and unchangeable. The idea that the tests may have been biased in such a way as to allow and even encourage these interpretations was not readily recognised.

We will return to this issue in Chapter 2 where we will examine the controversy about whether or not intelligence is innate, and how one should interpret the supposed differences in intelligence scores between social groups. In fact, as you will find out, in the decade after Binet's death, his noble aim of using intelligence testing to help children who struggle at school was abandoned, and measuring intelligence was transformed into a tool of oppression and discrimination. However, before we delve into this controversy, let us consider in more detail some of the principles behind intelligence measurement. We will start with the concept of the intelligence quotient or IQ in Section 3.

Summary

- Alfred Binet was the author of the first modern test of intelligence – the Binet–Simon test.

- Binet's aim was to create a test that could be used to identify children with special educational needs, by reliably measuring a child's ability in relation to their peers.

- Binet was a firm believer in the power of education, and advocated that in the right environment, with the right support, children who seem unable to benefit from schooling can be helped to overcome their problems.

- The structure and content of the Binet–Simon test strongly influenced the development of most subsequent intelligence tests.

3   The IQ and the distribution of ability

As we have seen in the Binet–Simon test, and this is true of most subsequent intelligence tests, a variety of very different tasks involving words, numbers, drawings, abstract reasoning and so on were used to derive an overall measure of intellectual level. One of Binet's contemporaries, the British psychologist Charles Spearman, argued that this is a valid approach because people who perform well on one set of reasoning tasks (such as processing numbers), also tend to do well on others (such as processing words). Spearman (1904) suggested that these **correlations** indicate that there is an underlying factor that underpins performance on all the different tasks that make up an intelligence test. He called this factor 'general intelligence', commonly abbreviated to *g*.

The evidence for Spearman's conclusion about the existence of *g* was not particularly strong. It was based on a study of a small group of boys attending a preparatory school, which found that pupils who did well in one set of subjects, such as English or French, also did well in others, such as maths (Richardson, 1991). Nonetheless, the notion of a singular 'general intelligence' has stuck, and has been implicit in most intelligence tests since (Richardson, 1998). It lies at the core of the concept of IQ, the intelligence quotient, which has become synonymous with the very notion of intelligence.

3.1   Calculating the IQ

The IQ, which stands for **intelligence quotient**, was first proposed in the early twentieth century by the German psychologist William Stern. You read in Section 2.2 that Binet assessed intelligence by looking at a child's mental age in relation to their chronological age. Stern believed this to be somewhat imprecise. It was difficult to make direct comparisons about intelligence across children of different ages, for example. Stern wanted to find a way of encapsulating intelligence in a single number in such a way that would allow easy comparisons. This number is the IQ.

Stern's formula for calculating IQ involved simply dividing the mental age (as indicated by test performance) by the chronological age (Gould, 1996). For example, imagine the case of a 4-year-old whose test performance was comparable to that of an average 6-year-old. Using Stern's formula their IQ would be calculated as follows: 6 (mental age)

Correlation

A measure of an association between two events or things. In the case of an intelligence test, this means that those who perform well on one task will also do well on another.

g, or general intelligence

The factor believed to underpin performance on different tasks in an intelligence test.

Intelligence quotient (IQ)

A score on an intelligence test which indicates how a person's intellectual ability compares to the general population.

divided by 4 (chronological age), gives the score, the IQ, of 1.50. However, a few years after Stern put forward this formula, Lewis Terman, the author of the Stanford–Binet test, proposed that the ratio between mental and chronological age (1.50 in this example) should be multiplied by 100, effectively rounding up the IQ score (in this example to 150; Murdoch, 2007). So Terman's formula goes as follows:

$$IQ = \frac{\text{Mental age}}{\text{Chronological age}} \times 100$$

This formula states that IQ equals mental age divided by chronological age, multiplied by 100. It means that a child whose mental age is the same as their chronological age would have a score of 100. If the formula is applied to a child with a mental age of 8, and a chronological age of 8, what we have is 8 divided by 8, which equals 1, multiplied by 100 which equals 100. Therefore, a score of 100 *at any age* would indicate average performance. Any score above 100 indicates that a child demonstrates above-average intelligence for its age group (mental age is higher than chronological age), while any score below 100 suggests that the child is lagging behind its peers. Going back to the example which we looked at in Section 2.2, a 3-year-old whose performance was comparable to that of a 4-year-old would be said to have the mental age of 4, and an IQ of 133 (4/3 × 100 = 133), while a 5-year-old with the same performance on an intelligence test (and therefore the same mental age) would obtain the IQ score of 80 (4/5 × 100 = 80). The main advantage of this formula is that, unlike Stern's original one, it produces whole numbers, without decimal points, while still making it easy to compare the intelligence of children regardless of age.

Although there is a tentative link between the concept of IQ and Binet's idea of comparing a child's mental and chronological age, it should be pointed out that Binet was vehemently opposed to the use of IQ as a measure of intelligence. He feared that IQ makes intelligence testing and measurement seem a lot more precise than it actually was, and that it leads people to accept that human abilities can be reduced to a single score. Also, for Binet, intelligence testing was useful only as a rough diagnostic tool for identifying children with special needs; he did not believe that it should be used for ranking all children in terms of ability. Finally, he believed that the popularisation of IQ as a measure of intelligence makes intelligence seem like a fixed, inborn quality, rather than something that can be changed through education (Gould, 1996).

As you will see in Chapter 2, developments in intelligence testing after Binet's death demonstrated that he was right on all three counts.

One thing you may have noticed is that Terman's formula for calculating IQ is derived from tests developed for children. The ratio between mental and chronological age is relevant only during the period of development, when age is closely correlated with the ability to perform mental tasks: most children, unlike adults, naturally get better at reasoning tasks as they get older. In most adults, the notion of 'mental age' holds very little value. Although IQ tends to change throughout a lifetime, the standards for assessing a 40-year-old and a 30-year-old, for example, are the same. So how is IQ calculated for adults? To answer this question, it is necessary to introduce the concept of normal distribution.

3.2   Normal distribution of intelligence

Normal distribution
The assumption that characteristics which vary between people will be distributed across the population in such a way that values at or close to the average will be more frequent than extreme ones.

Normal distribution refers to the assumption that human characteristics which vary between people – including things like height and shoe size, but also some specific abilities such as the capacity to remember a string of random numbers – will be distributed in a population (e.g. children of the same age, people of the same gender, or citizens of the same country) in such a way that values at or close to the average will occur more frequently than extreme ones. For example, if the average shoe size for men in the UK is 9, we can assume that most people will require shoes within a size or two of this number, while the very small or very large sizes (6 or 12, for example) will be comparatively rare among men in the UK. In fact, the more extreme the size, the rarer it will be in the population. Knowing that something is *normally distributed* can be very useful. Shoe manufacturers and retailers, for example, use it to estimate the demand for different sizes, and to plan their stock.

One of the fundamental assumptions of intelligence measurement is that intelligence too is normally distributed; that most people's score will be close to the average and fewer people will have more extreme scores. Represented graphically, normal distribution looks like a bell, which is why it is sometimes referred to as the 'bell curve' (see Figure 1.4).

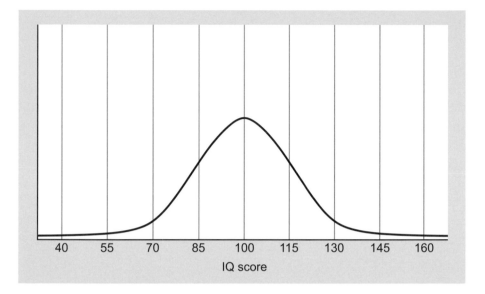

Figure 1.4   The 'bell curve': normal distribution of IQ

Activity 1.2

Have a closer look at Figure 1.4, which shows the normal distribution of IQ scores. How would you explain what the graph shows to another person?

The first thing to note is that the horizontal line across the bottom of the graph (known as the x-axis) displays the range of IQ scores, ranging from 40 to 160. The vertical line on the left of the graph (the y-axis) represents the frequency with which each score occurs in the population. As you can see, the curve rises with the IQ score up until the midpoint (the IQ score of 100), and then it descends again. This means that the IQ scores of around 100 are the most common in the population and that the further away a score is from the average, the less likely it is to occur.

Note that in IQ measurement, the score at which the bell curve reaches the highest point is always 100. As you read in Section 3.1, according to Terman's formula for calculating IQ in children, 100 always denotes the norm (the average), regardless of age. In adult tests, the same number is used to represent average intelligence. So, there is nothing magical about the number 100 – it is simply a convenient figure for representing scores above the norm (higher than 100) or below the norm (lower than 100). Also because all tests use IQ of 100 as the mean, scores can be easily compared across different tests.

In addition to setting the average score (the top of the curve) at 100, there is a further assumption about IQ tests that follows directly from the precise shape of the bell curve. You can see this in Figure 1.5. The shape of the curve indicates that just over two-thirds of people within a population (68.3 per cent to be more precise) will have an IQ score between 85 and 115 (the area shaded in light grey in Figure 1.5) and that just over 95 per cent will have an IQ between 70 and 130. By extension, fewer than one in 40 people (2.3 per cent) will have an IQ score lower than 70, and the same proportion will have an IQ higher than 130 (the two dark grey areas near the 'tails' of the bell curve).

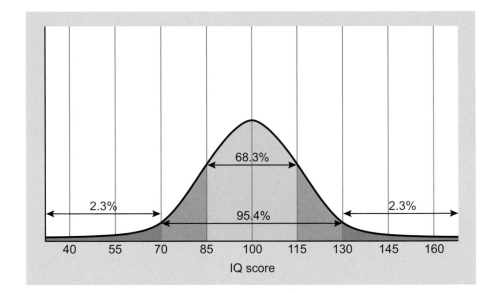

Figure 1.5   Normal distribution of IQ (with percentages)

The assumption that intelligence is normally distributed is enshrined in the design of IQ tests. When new tests are created, or existing ones updated, items are selected and the scoring calibrated and modified so that the average score is 100 and the distribution of scores resembles the bell curve, with its distinctive, symmetrical shape.

Conceptualising intelligence in this way has distinct advantages. One is that as soon as a person's score is calculated, it is possible to say where they are placed in relation to the population as a whole: whether their intelligence is average, whether they are in the top (or bottom) 5, 10 or 20 per cent of the population. Also, the IQ score is useful for comparing performance across different versions of IQ tests. But most importantly, the basic concept of IQ is remarkably simple and its ability to reduce human intelligence to a single number has undoubtedly contributed to its persistence and popularity. When the media report that some historical figure or celebrity had 'an IQ of 165' this requires little elaboration: many people, even if they have never studied psychology or seen the bell curve, will understand that this indicates high intelligence and points to rare genius.

However, it is important to bear in mind that the idea that intelligence is normally distributed, in the precise way implied by the bell curve, has never actually been demonstrated. It is no more than an assumption, first put forward by Galton in the nineteenth century. Galton's thinking was guided by evidence from medical records that things like height and chest size were normally distributed. He simply assumed that what would be true of physical properties would also apply to intellectual abilities. This supposition was later endorsed by other researchers and practitioners, and has remained the fundamental, albeit untested, assumption in intelligence measurement, built into each and every intelligence test. This is why the IQ score should never be seen as an 'absolute' measure of intelligence. It is simply an indication of how a person's performance at a set of tasks compares to the norms thought to apply to the population with which they belong.

Summary

- Intelligence testing is based on the assumption that performance on a range of reasoning and problem-solving tasks is underpinned by an underlying factor, namely *intelligence*.

- IQ or intelligence quotient is a way of expressing numerically how a person's performance on a set of tasks in an intelligence test compares to the norms thought to apply to the population with which they belong.

- IQ tests are designed so that values at or close to the average will occur more frequently than extreme ones. This is called *normal distribution*. The score of 100 always represents the average on an IQ test.

4   The anatomy of an intelligence test

In this section, we will examine in more detail the structure and content of an intelligence test, using as an example what is probably the most widely used intelligence test in the world today: the Wechsler Adult Intelligence Scale, or WAIS. The first version of this scale was developed in 1939 by the American psychologist David Wechsler. The original version was called the Wechsler–Bellevue Intelligence Scale, after the Bellevue Hospital in New York, where Wechsler worked in the 1930s. However, the test has been updated a number of times since then, and the second edition was released in 1955 under the new name, the Wechsler Adult Intelligence Scale. The most recent, fourth, edition of the test (the WAIS-IV) was released in 2008. Unlike the Binet–Simon test, introduced in Section 2, which was designed to measure children's intellectual abilities, the Wechsler scale was originally developed specifically to measure adult intelligence. There is, however, also a separate Wechsler Intelligence Scale for Children, which was first developed in 1944. The most recent edition of this test was released in 2003 (WISC-IV).

It is worth noting that the WAIS is neither the only nor in any way the 'authoritative' test of intelligence. Nevertheless, the worldwide popularity of the WAIS makes it a convenient example for examining what an instrument used to measure intelligence actually looks like.

4.1   The Wechsler Adult Intelligence Scale (WAIS-IV)

The current version of the Wechsler scale consists of ten core subtests which are used for calculating the IQ. Because the WAIS-IV is protected by copyright (see Box 1.1), it is not possible to reproduce the items featured in the test so we will provide examples similar to those which are actually used (these are adapted from Deary, 2001).

Box 1.1   Intelligence tests and copyright

There are several reasons why those who own the rights to intelligence scales – these are mainly large companies dedicated to developing psychological tests – are keen to retain control over their intellectual property. First, they have a commercial interest: they earn money through the sale of the tests. In that respect they

---

operate like any other private company. Second, intelligence tests need to be updated and standardised, and this is very expensive. The income generated by the sale of the tests covers the extensive costs of research and development.

A third reason for limiting access to tests is that if people could easily obtain the actual items used in the WAIS, they could learn the answers and in doing so improve their score. For those who believe in the usefulness of IQ tests, this presents a problem: free access to tests would effectively undermine their validity as a measure of intelligence.

Fourth, administering a complex test such as the WAIS-IV requires extensive training. The WAIS, and similar tests, are supposed to be administered only by specially trained and licensed professionals, usually clinical or educational psychologists, who engage on a one-to-one basis with the person being tested. Their assessment of that person's ability would be informed not just by the test scores, but also by observations made in the testing session. For example, they would look at whether the person was nervous or distracted, as well as how they actually approached the different tasks. Restrictions placed on the availability and use of the tests represent one way of ensuring that they are administered only by qualified practitioners with the skills and knowledge needed to interpret the results.

However, not all IQ tests available on the market are as complex and time-consuming to administer as the WAIS. A number of abbreviated, simplified tests have been developed in recent years, which can even be administered by telephone, by post or over the internet. While these tests offer the advantage of expediency and are cheaper to administer than the WAIS, they lack the kind of insight into a person's ability that a testing session with a qualified professional offers. That is why the results of the simplified tests need to be treated with greater caution, and why, when interpreting research findings about human intelligence, it is important to bear in mind what kind of test researchers used.

You will find out more about the administration of the Wechsler test and the interpretation of results in the film *Intelligence testing: practical applications*, which is available on the module website.

The WAIS assesses a range of skills which are thought to be underpinned by general intelligence. In the most recent version, the ten core subtests are divided into four components: (1) verbal comprehension; (2) perceptual reasoning; (3) working memory; and (4) processing speed. Each subtest contains between 14 and 33 questions, which range from easy to quite challenging. Like in the Binet–Simon test, these are presented in order of difficulty and the testing on each

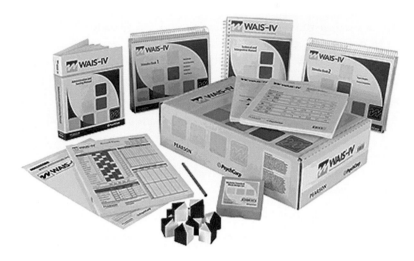

Figure 1.6   The kit needed to administer the WAIS-IV test. Image Copyright © 2008 NCS Pearson, Inc. Reproduced with permission. All rights reserved.

subtest ends when the person completing it can no longer manage the task.

Let's look at each of the four components of the WAIS.

- **Verbal comprehension**. This involves three subtests which measure general verbal skills, such as the ability to understand and use words. The test taker will be asked, for example, to interpret the meaning of a word (e.g. 'chair', 'hesitant', 'presumptuous'), identify what two words have in common (e.g. 'apple' and 'pear'; 'painting' and 'symphony'), or answer general knowledge questions (e.g. 'What is the capital of France?', 'Name three oceans', 'Who wrote the book *Inferno*?').

- **Perceptual reasoning**. This involves three subtests which measure non-verbal reasoning, for example the ability to manipulate images, reproduce patterns, solve problems, etc. The subtests involve picture puzzles rather than words. In one of them the test taker is shown identical blocks with surfaces of solid red, surfaces of solid white, and surfaces that are half red and half white. As part of the test, they are required to use the blocks to reproduce a pattern that the tester presents to them (you can see these blocks at the bottom of Figure 1.6).

Working memory
The kind of memory that is used for temporarily storing and managing information required to carry out a task. You will learn about working memory in Part 3 of the module.

- **Working memory**. Two subtests measure a person's **working memory**, that is, the part of memory that temporarily holds a limited amount of information needed to carry out a task. One of the subtests involves repeating a sequence of between two and nine numbers read out by the tester. The other involves completing simple mental arithmetic.

- **Processing speed**. Performance on these two subtests is timed to assess the speed and accuracy of processing visual information. In one of the subtests, the test taker is presented with a row of abstract symbols (e.g. ☒ ◎ ➤ ▫ + ♪) and a pair of symbols (e.g. ➤ ▢), only one of which is featured in the row. The task is to identify which of the pair appears in the row of symbols. This task is not in itself complicated, but it is the speed that counts: the person administering the test is examining how many of these the test taker can complete successfully in 90 seconds.

Activity 1.3

Take another look at the kind of tasks involved in the WAIS-IV. What sort of skills are being assessed, and how similar are these to the skills assessed in the Binet–Simon test? Does it seem to you as if they measure the same thing? To what extent do these tasks measure what you think intelligence is?

The WAIS-IV assesses a variety of mental functions: some subtests involve numbers and words, others focus on processing abstract symbols and shapes. Some test general knowledge, others measure the ability to spot patterns or figure out rules. This kind of variation is quite typical of IQ tests, and we saw it in the Binet–Simon test too. However, one aspect of intelligence explicitly measured in WAIS that we did not see in the Binet–Simon test is the speed of processing, and this reflects a subsequent development in intelligence research.

So what do the different tasks that make up the WAIS have in common? When intelligence tests are developed, the fact that tasks may not be *obviously* related is not as important as the fact that scores on them tend to be correlated. Just like Spearman argued more than a century ago, people who do well on one type of task, tend to do well on others, and what underlies this similarity in performance is assumed to be intelligence. In the case of WAIS-IV, the performance on the ten core subtests is used to calculate an overall intelligence score – a measure of a person's IQ.

The assumption that people who do well on one subtest will do well on others applies to people *generally*. It does not mean that everyone's processing speed will be as good (or as bad) as their verbal comprehension, or that working memory is always correlated with general knowledge. This is why the overall IQ is an imperfect measure. The WAIS-IV recognises this, to some extent. As well as calculating an overall IQ score, the test produces four 'index scores' which correspond to the four components of the test: verbal comprehension, perceptual reasoning, working memory and processing speed. So, once a person has completed the test, the tester might conclude, for example, that their IQ is close to average (95), but that they have an exceptionally high perceptual reasoning index score (120), which in terms of the ability to organise and solve non-verbal problems places them in the top 10 per cent of the population. Or that they have a very low working memory index score (75), which might alert the psychologist to a specific deficit in this aspect of intelligence.

The fact that index scores are calculated alongside the general IQ suggests that, according to the current version of the Wechsler scale, the structure of human intelligence is more complex than the idea of a 'general intelligence' would suggest. The four different specific abilities, although related, are deemed to be sufficiently distinct to warrant a separate 'index score' (see Figure 1.7).

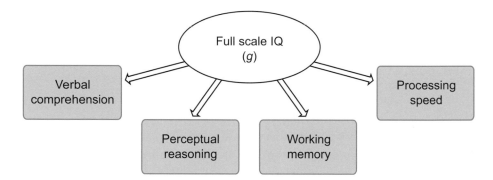

Figure 1.7   The structure of intelligence according to the WAIS-IV

This opens up the question that has puzzled intelligence researchers for a long time: should we conceptualise human intelligence as a single construct, or would it be more appropriate to talk of 'multiple intelligences'?

4.2   One intelligence or multiple intelligences?

Among researchers on intelligence there is widespread and long-standing agreement that human intellectual abilities have a complex structure. Even Spearman, who first proposed the idea of *g*, argued that intelligence is composed of different – but related – specific abilities. Also, ever since Binet, psychologists have made the distinction between verbal and non-verbal components of intelligence in recognition that not all of human intellectual ability involves language. In fact, prior to the most recent version of the Wechsler scale (with its four 'index scores'), the WAIS was divided into just two components – the verbal and non-verbal subtests – in recognition of this basic structure of intelligence.

Over the past century, other distinctions have been proposed, in most instances involving between two and eight components of intelligence (e.g. Thurstone, 1938; Carrol, 1993). Particularly noteworthy is the now highly influential distinction between fluid and crystallised intelligence, suggested in the 1970s by Raymond Cattell. **Fluid intelligence** is believed to include abilities like logical thinking and problem solving, which are independent of acquired knowledge, while **crystallised intelligence** refers to aspects of intelligence dependent on experience, such as language ability and general knowledge (Cattell, 1971).

The disagreements over the precise structure of intellectual abilities are important because they point to a broader issue with intelligence research and measurement. What we know about intelligence, and its structure, does not stem from a well-developed **theory** about how the human mind works, or about why people differ in their abilities, which then informs the construction of intelligence tests (Deary, 2001). Instead, the general approach has been to first build the tests that measure differences in performance on a range of mental tasks, and then use the results to infer what the ability underpinning this performance (i.e. 'intelligence') might be, and how it is organised.

The implication of this is that the question of whether intelligence is a single phenomenon or not has been, by and large, a *technical* one: psychologists have debated the structure of intelligence while knowing very little about what the different components mean, what it is that connects them, or indeed why they may be important to people's everyday functioning in the real world (Richardson, 1998). In the simplest of terms, the tests appear to be measuring something, but precisely *what* this is remains less clear.

This issue is important in the light of the fact, noted in the Introduction, that there is little agreement among researchers about what intelligence is, beyond the idea that it underpins differences between people in particular abilities and performance. But the crucial

Fluid intelligence
The ability to think logically and solve problems, which is independent of acquired knowledge or experience. We will examine how fluid intelligence might be measured in Chapter 3 of *Investigating Intelligence*.

Crystallised intelligence
The ability to apply acquired skills, knowledge and experience to novel situations.

Theory
A set of propositions about a psychological phenomenon (e.g. intelligence) which forms the basis of an explanation.

question is performance at *what*? What is it that people who score high in intelligence tests are better at? This is the question we turn to next.

4.3 The question of validity: what do intelligence tests actually measure?

In Section 3.2 we used the analogy with shoe size to illustrate the idea that intelligence is assumed to be normally distributed. There is, however, a very important difference between a physical property such as shoe size and a psychological construct like intelligence. Shoe size is something that can be measured directly by measuring the length of a foot. Thus, there is no uncertainty about what a shoe size is a measure of.

It is quite a different issue when we are dealing with psychological phenomena that we cannot observe or measure directly. How do we know that an intelligence test actually measures ability, and not something else, such as the effects of practice? How do we know what the IQ is a measure of?

Validity
The extent to which a test measures what it has been designed to measure. You will learn more about validity in Chapter 7 of *Investigating Methods*.

This is a question that has plagued research on intelligence since its inception. In psychology, this is known as the question of **validity**, that is, the extent to which a test measures what it sets out to measure. Galton was aware of it at the time when he was testing people in his 'anthropometric laboratory' in London. In fact it was Galton who provided the solution that still holds in much of intelligence research: the only way to ensure that an intelligence test is valid is to compare it 'with an independent measure of [intellectual] powers' (Galton, cited in Richardson, 1998, p. 102). In other words, you need to find someone who you already believe to be 'intelligent', and someone who you believe is not, give them the test, and if the expected difference between these people is reflected in the scores, you can conclude that the test measures intelligence.

Activity 1.4
Take a closer look at the solution proposed by Galton. What would you say is its main limitation?

You may have spotted a problem with Galton's approach: it assumes that even before an intelligence test is developed, it is necessary to have some preconceived notion about who is intelligent and who is not. Traditionally, researchers developing tests for assessing children have linked intelligence with school performance as an 'obvious' measure of ability: an intelligence test would be considered valid if it discriminates between children who do well at school and those who do not.

The link with school performance is the criterion that Binet used in his work. In designing their test, Binet and Simon needed to ensure that children who were good at the Binet–Simon test, also performed well at school, while those who were poor at these tasks tended to struggle. Now, in Binet's case, it could be argued that this approach was justified, given that his main aim was to identify children who struggle at school. But other researchers who came after Binet, and who used IQ tests as a general measure of ability, have followed the same principle.

And yet, the premise about the link between intelligence and educational performance is fraught with problems. One of the reasons why intelligence tests appear to be correlated with school performance is because they assess the kind of abilities that children develop at school and because schools teach skills which make people better at intelligence tests. If schools prepare pupils for the 11-plus, or a similar intelligence-based entrance exam, then they are effectively teaching them the skills needed to perform well on an IQ test. Put differently, it may be that it is not some underlying intellectual ability, or 'intelligence', that causes children to do well at school, but rather that activity at school enables them to do well in IQ tests.

Also, recent research has shown that when it comes to predicting school performance, the most important factor is not the IQ, but the extent of parental involvement in a child's education. In fact, the IQ score itself has been shown to be closely linked to levels of parental interest in a child's learning, parents' involvement in play, whether or not they motivate or 'push' their children, and so on (Mackintosh, 2011). Similarly, a recent study by Duckworth et al. (2011) found that material incentives improved the performance on IQ tests by, on average, 10 points. This suggests that performance on intelligence tests is also influenced by motivation.

All these findings point to the possibility that intelligence tests may not, in fact, measure some basic mental ability that differentiates the intrinsically clever from those who are not. Performance on the tests is, in fact, a function of a broader range of factors, including a person's social environment, their relationship with people around them, their view of themselves and others, and their drive, motivation, initiative and confidence, as well as prior exposure to the kind of tasks that are featured in an IQ test (Richardson, 2002). All of these factors are linked to culture, social status and economic power, and not just to some abstract notion of 'intelligence'. This is a theme that we will be returning to in subsequent chapters.

Summary

- The Wechsler Adult Intelligence Scale (WAIS) is one of the most widely used tests today. It consists of ten subscales which assess four different components of intelligence: verbal comprehension, perceptual reasoning, working memory and processing speed.

- There is considerable debate among psychologists about whether intelligence is a single construct, or whether it would be more meaningful to talk about multiple intelligences. The most widely used distinction is between verbal and non-verbal intelligence.

- Traditionally, the validity of intelligence tests has been judged by how strongly they correlate with school performance.

- There is strong evidence that performance on IQ tests is linked to a broader range of factors, including a person's social environment, their self-esteem, motivation and initiative, and their experience.

5   Conclusion

In this chapter, we examined the basic principles behind intelligence measurement. First we looked at the early history of intelligence testing, specifically Binet's efforts to move beyond the problematic assumptions of craniometry and develop a psychological test that could be used to assess children's intellectual development and educational needs. Then we looked at how, over time, intelligence measurement gradually became more sophisticated, with the development of the concept of IQ and the principle of normal distribution. We also explored what a typical intelligence test looks like and considered some of the debates about the structure of human intelligence. As you read, there is considerable disagreement among researchers about the precise structure of human intellectual functioning and about whether the idea of single, general 'intelligence' or *g* is as useful as the conventional understanding of intelligence might imply.

However, probably the biggest challenge of intelligence testing is that human intellectual functioning cannot be measured directly. This points to an important paradox at the centre of intelligence research. The need for an intelligence test stems from the idea that there is such a thing as 'intelligence' that can be measured. At the same time, the only way of getting at intelligence, and addressing the question of what it is, is through psychological measurement. This conundrum has given rise to important questions about the nature of intelligence, and more importantly, about what it is that tests of intelligence *actually* measure. Do they assess intrinsic ability, or the effects of things like culture, social status or experience?

This question lies at the core of the issue which we will consider in the next chapter, namely why people differ in intellectual ability. This is where intelligence research has proved most controversial. As you will find out, in the early twentieth century intelligence testing was transformed from what Binet envisaged as the means of helping children who struggle at school, into a tool for legitimising inequality, discrimination and racism in society. The outcome of this development was one of the darkest chapters in the history of psychology.

References

Aiken, L. R. and Groth-Marnat, G. (2006) *Psychological Testing and Assessment*, 12th edn, Boston, MA, Pearson.

Carroll, J. B. (1993) *Human Cognitive Abilities: A Survey of Factor-Analytic Studies*, Cambridge, Cambridge University Press.

Cattell, R. B. (1971) *Abilities: Their Structure, Growth, and Action*, New York, NY, Houghton Mifflin.

Deary, I. J. (2001) *Intelligence: A Very Short Introduction*, Oxford, Oxford University Press.

Duckworth, A. L., Quinn, P. Q., Lynam, D. R., Loeberd, R. and Stouthamer-Loeber, M. (2011) 'Role of test motivation in intelligence testing', *Proceedings of the National Academy of Sciences*, vol. 108, pp. 7716–20.

Gould, S. J. (1996) *The Mismeasure of Man*, Revised and Expanded Edition, London, Penguin.

Mackintosh, N. J. (2011) 'Intelligence and its measurement: 1. History of theories and measurement of intelligence', in Sternberg, R. J. and Kaufman, S. B. (eds) *The Cambridge Handbook of Intelligence*, Cambridge, Cambridge University Press.

Murdoch, S. (2007) *IQ: A Smart History of a Failed Idea*, Hoboken, NJ, John Wiley & Sons.

Richardson, K. (1991) *Understanding Intelligence*, Buckingham, Open University Press.

Richardson, K. (1998) *The Origins of Human Potential: Evolution, Development and Psychology*, London, Routledge.

Richardson, K. (2002) 'What IQ tests test', *Theory & Psychology*, vol. 12, no. 3, pp. 283–314.

Rosenthal, R. (1966) *Experimenter Effects in Behavioral Research*, New York, NY, Appleton-Century-Crofts.

Spearman, C. (1904) 'General intelligence: objectively determined and measured', *American Journal of Psychology*, vol. 15, pp. 201–93.

Thurstone, L. L. (1938) *Primary Mental Abilities*, Chicago, Ill, University of Chicago Press.

Chapter 2
Explaining differences in intelligence

Contents

Aims and objectives

After studying this chapter you should be able to:

- outline the main controversies surrounding research on intelligence and the interpretations of why people differ in performance on IQ tests

- describe Robert Yerkes's study on the intelligence of US Army recruits and identify the main shortcoming of the study

- appreciate the dangers of cultural and class bias in intelligence testing

- describe what *heritability* means

- identify the advantages and disadvantages of some of the methods that have been used to study the heritability of intelligence.

1 Introduction

In 1994, the American Psychological Association (APA) – the main professional body representing psychologists in the United States – established a special task force which was asked to produce a comprehensive and up-to-date report on 'the knowns and unknowns' about human intelligence (Neisser et al., 1996). It is quite rare for a professional body like the APA to commission leading scholars to review areas of psychological research in this way. This unusual move was in response to the publication, in the same year, of the controversial book *The Bell Curve* by two American authors, Richard Herrnstein and Charles Murray. The book contained a number of highly contentious claims. Two of them caused particularly strong public reaction. First, the authors argued that differences in IQ have a strong genetic basis and are therefore fixed, and that environmental factors, including education, make little difference to the development of a person's intellectual ability. Second, they argued that there are inherent differences in intelligence between social groups, particularly across class and racial divisions. As these group differences, in Herrnstein's and Murray's (1994) view, were also genetic, they too were seen as permanent and unalterable.

In itself, Herrnstein and Murray's work does not warrant any degree of attention. The authors' claims, and their political agenda, have been discredited, and the book is today remembered for the controversy it caused rather than any soundness in the research behind it (Gould, 1996). However, the reaction to *The Bell Curve* and the creation of APA's task force suggest that the book touched a raw nerve within the psychological profession. It provoked psychologists to recognise that there is an important *political* skeleton in the closet of intelligence research, one which, unless it is dealt with appropriately, will continue to reappear and will threaten to bring the whole discipline into disrepute.

In this chapter, we will examine in more detail two related questions that lie at the core of the controversy surrounding intelligence: What is the origin of the perceived differences in intellectual ability, whether between individuals, or between groups? Are these differences reducible to 'nature' and genetics, or are they caused by 'nurture', that is, by environmental factors such as differences in culture, experience, social status and educational opportunities?

The central dilemma here, namely whether an aspect of human psychology is determined by inherited (genetic) predispositions, or whether it is influenced by culture and the environment, is one that permeates the discipline of psychology. You will encounter other examples of the 'nature/nurture' debate later in the module, as well as throughout your study of psychology. What is distinct about intelligence, however, is that because of the subject matter – human intellectual ability – the nature/nurture question inescapably acquires political significance.

We will start the chapter by critically examining the proposition that there are inherent group differences in intelligence. We will do so by looking at one of the most influential, but also most contentious, studies in the history of intelligence research: the army testing programme carried out during 1917–18 by a team of American psychologists led by Robert Yerkes. There are good reasons for looking at this study in particular. As you will see, it not only provides a useful historical lesson about what happens when political biases guide scientific research and the interpretation of findings, but it also shows how the nature of intelligence measurement changed in the second decade of the twentieth century. Alfred Binet's mission to use intelligence tests for assessing an individual child's educational needs gave way to a different set of concerns, namely mass testing of children and adults for purposes of selection and screening.

You read about Alfred Binet in Chapter 1, Section 2 of Investigating Intelligence.

Summary

- Intelligence is a controversial topic because of attempts by some authors to argue that there are innate differences in intelligence between groups in society.

- The 'nature/nurture' debate in psychology refers to the question of whether inherited (genetic) predispositions or environmental influences are more important in the development of psychological phenomena.

2 The emergence of mass testing of intelligence

In Chapter 1, you read that in 1908 the American psychologist Henry Goddard took the Binet–Simon test from Paris to the United States, where it was eventually developed by Lewis Terman into the Stanford–Binet test.

Initially, the ideas that Goddard brought back with him from Europe were not well received in the United States. Psychology was still a young discipline then, and the general public was uncertain about its ability to reliably measure aspects of the human mind (Murdoch, 2007). Most American psychologists were similarly unconvinced by the idea of mental testing. At the time, measuring intellectual ability was of interest mainly to doctors and educators, who were the ones diagnosing people with learning disabilities.

In Chapter 3 of *Investigating Intelligence* we will consider in more detail the role of intelligence testing in the diagnosis of learning disability.

Intelligence testing was also gradually being taken up by the immigration authorities, who were keen to prevent 'mentally unfit' immigrants from settling in the United States (see Box 2.1). However, it was only in the aftermath of the First World War that this area of research captured the imagination of the psychological profession and the general public in the United States. As we shall see, this development is closely tied up with one of the most controversial studies of intelligence.

Box 2.1

Between 1892 and 1924, over 12 million immigrants to the United States were processed at Ellis Island, located off the coast of Manhattan in New York. As part of the screening process, immigration officials looked out for a long list of medical conditions and physical disabilities which the US government had decided made people ineligible for residence in the country. People afflicted by these conditions were simply turned away, and sent back to their place of origin.

Over the years, those running Ellis Island realised that while officials were generally good at spotting physical disabilities, they were not as good at screening people with learning disabilities, who the government was also keen to exclude. In the 1910s, under the leadership of a doctor by the name of Howard Knox, specific tests were developed to identify the 'mentally unfit'. By today's standards, these tests were crude and unsophisticated, but they followed the basic principles of intelligence measurement. They aimed to measure performance on a set of generic reasoning tasks, with the aim of assessing a person's overall intellectual ability (Boake, 2002).

Figure 2.1   Howard Knox (left) testing an immigrant at Ellis Island

The testing procedures at Ellis Island were lengthy and complex. The immigrants were tested individually, often in the presence of an interpreter. This meant that long queues of passengers, already exhausted by the difficult boat journey across the Atlantic, had to wait for hours to undergo yet another examination, in the hope that they would pass and be allowed to begin a new life in the United States.

Although Knox's contribution to the history of intelligence testing is often overlooked, his work on Ellis Island is important as the first example of the mass use of intelligence tests for purposes of screening.

2.1 Robert Yerkes and the army testing programme

The declaration of war on Germany by the United States in 1917 brought about the mass mobilisation of the US Army. At the time, many psychologists felt that while other professions – doctors, nurses, scientists, engineers, etc. – were applying their skills to help the war effort, psychology was lagging behind. This troubled Robert Yerkes, the then president of the APA. He believed that psychology must seize 'the opportunity to do something important' for the military, and in doing so demonstrate the relevance of psychology to society (Yerkes, cited in Murdoch, 2007, p. 70). Yerkes believed that the solution lay in measuring intelligence: by introducing intelligence testing into the process of military recruitment, the army could screen out those whose low intellectual ability would be an impediment to performance on the battlefield. Psychology, he believed, could make the army more effective.

Figure 2.2 Members of the Committee on the Psychological Examination of Recruits which developed the army mental tests. Robert Yerkes is in the second row, in the middle. In front of him, holding a camera, is Henry Goddard. Lewis Terman is in the second row, furthest to the right

Yerkes's original plan was to test recruits one at a time, in the same way that Knox was testing immigrants at Ellis Island. But the US Army, an institution that wanted speed and efficiency, objected to this. So, in the spring of 1917, with the help of colleagues (including Henry Goddard and Lewis Terman), Yerkes developed the first pen-and-paper versions of an intelligence test, which could be administered to a large number of people at the same time (Gould, 1996). These became known as the 'army mental tests' (Yoakum and Yerkes, 1920).

2.2   Army Alpha and Beta tests

The army mental tests consisted of two versions: Alpha and Beta. The completion of the Alpha test required basic reading ability, so it was intended for literate recruits with a good command of the English language. The rest (including the poor, most of whom were illiterate, and members of the country's large immigrant communities) were given the Beta test, which involved pictures and numbers, rather than words.

The Alpha test developed by Yerkes and his team included eight subtests, which assessed a similar kind of abilities to most IQ tests today. For example, the recruits were tested on their vocabulary, general knowledge, the ability to solve arithmetical problems, and so on. Each subtest included between 20 and 40 items, which were presented in ascending order of difficulty. Examples of each of the subtests are provided in Table 2.1.

The Beta test, aimed at recruits who were illiterate or did not speak English well, comprised seven subtests. These included creating patterns from cardboard pieces, comparing strings of numbers, and identifying the missing feature from a picture of a familiar object (see Table 2.2).

Table 2.1 Examples of items used in the army Alpha test

Test 1: Oral directions The task was to complete a series of commands or directions as quickly as possible.	Make a figure 2 in the second circle and also a cross in the third circle (5 seconds) ○ ○ ○ ○ ○ Cross out the letter just after F and also draw a line under the second letter after I (10 seconds) A B C D E F G H I J K L M N O P
Test 2: Arithmetical problems	How many are 30 men and 7 men? (Answer: 37 men) If it takes 6 men 3 days to dig a 180-foot drain, how many men are needed to dig it in half a day? (Answer: 36 men)
Test 3: Practical judgement	Cats are useful because: a) they catch mice, b) they are gentle, c) they are afraid of dogs? (Answer: a) they catch mice) Why is wheat better for food than corn? Because a) it is more nutritious, b) it is more expensive, c) it can be ground finer? (Answer: a) it is more nutritious)
Test 4: Synonym-antonym The task was to indicate if two words mean the same thing (synonyms) or the opposite things (antonyms).	wet–dry (Answer: opposite) extinguish–quench (Answer: same) dissension–harmony (Answer: opposite)
Test 5: Disarranged sentences The task was to indicate whether a meaningful sentence could be constructed from a string of words.	not eat gunpowder to good is (Answer: true, 'gunpowder is not good to eat') and eat good gold silver to are (Answer: false)
Test 6: Number series completion	3, 4, 5, 6, 7, 8, _, _ (Answer 9, 10) 29, 28, 26, 23, 19, 14, _, _ (Answer 8, 1)
Test 7: Analogies	Gun – shoots, knife – a) run, b) cuts, c) hat, d) bird (Answer: b) cuts) Moon – earth, earth – a) ground, b) Mars, c) sun, d) sky (Answer: c) sun)
Test 8: Information	The author of *The Raven* is: a) Stevenson, b) Kipling, c) Hawthorne, d) Poe) (Answer: d) Poe) Emeralds are usually: a) red, b) blue, c) green, d) yellow (Answer: c) green)

Source: Yoakum and Yerkes, 1920

Table 2.2 Examples of items used in the army Beta test

Test 1: Maze The task was to trace a path through the maze.	
Test 2: Cube analysis The task was to indicate how many cubes there are in a particular model (in this example, the answers are 2, 4, 6, 8 and 12).	
Test 3: X-O series The task was to enter Xs and Os in the remaining spaces, by establishing the pattern and completing the sequence.	
Test 4: Digit-symbol The task was to fill in the blank spaces under the numbers, by copying the appropriate symbol from the key.	
Test 5: Number checking The task was to compare two strings of numbers and determine whether they are same.	650 .... 650 041 .... 044 2579 .... 2579 3281 .... 3281 55190 .... 55102 39190 39190
Test 6: Picture completion The task was to correctly identify the missing feature from the familiar object. (In these examples, missing are: chimney, ear, filament and stamp.)	
Test 7: Geometrical construction The task was to manipulate a set of geometrical shapes to create a square.	

Source: Yoakum and Yerkes, 1920

As you read through the examples in Tables 2.1 and 2.2 you probably noticed the similarity between the tasks included in the two army mental tests and those featured in IQ tests today, including the Wechsler Adult Intelligence Scale (WAIS) which you read about in Chapter 1. This is not accidental. During the First World War, David Wechsler, who went on to create the WAIS, was part of Yerkes's team and was helping to administer the army tests. In the 1930s, when he began work on what was to become the WAIS, Wechsler embraced the basic principles of the army tests, and reused many of the items created by Yerkes and his team (Boake, 2002). Of course, the WAIS changed substantially over subsequent decades, but the visible similarities between the two tests are a reminder of this historical link between them, and an illustration of continuity in intelligence test design.

Activity 2.1

Take another look at the tasks illustrated in Tables 2.1 and 2.2. Would you say that the two versions of the army test, Alpha and Beta, measure the same thing? Would you say that what they measure is intelligence?

Yerkes maintained that the two tests did indeed measure the same thing, in spite of the differences between them. As a committed believer in the efficacy of the Alpha and Beta tests, he insisted that they both tapped into the same underlying factor, 'native intellectual ability', or intelligence (cited in Gould, 1996, p. 349). For example, he argued that the 'X-O series' task in the Beta test assesses the same ability as the 'number series completion' in the Alpha test (Yoakum and Yerkes, 1920). He was also convinced that performance on either test was unaffected by things like culture and educational opportunities, an issue that we will return to later.

Moreover, Yerkes maintained that the greatest advantage of mass testing was that it was extremely efficient. There was a time limit on each subtest, and overall the tests took less than an hour to complete. Based on their performance on either Alpha or Beta, each recruit was given a grade ranging from A to E (A indicating the highest level of intelligence, E the lowest). By the end of the war in 1918, as many as 1.7 million recruits had been tested, about half of the total number of men drafted into the US Army.

Figure 2.3   US Army recruits taking the Alpha test in 1917

2.3   From the army tests to educational selection

For the duration of Yerkes's project, the US military remained unconvinced about its usefulness. Only about 8000 men out of 1.7 million tested were relieved of military duties on the basis of low intelligence scores, a very small number considering the time and resources invested in the programme. Nevertheless, his employer's scepticism did not worry Yerkes. The sheer scale of the army testing programme and its high public profile ensured that psychology and intelligence measurement came out of the war with their reputations transformed (Murdoch, 2007). Yerkes made the most of the publicity generated by the army testing, and was able to convince both the members of his profession and the general public that intelligence can be measured, and that it is useful to do so. When Yerkes published the findings of his wartime research in 1921, he referred to the 'steady stream of requests from commercial concerns, educational institutions and individuals for the use of army methods' (Yerkes, 1921, p. 96). This marked the beginning of the era of the kind of commercialised mass mental testing that has been used ever since in education and job recruitment for purposes of selection.

The impact of the army testing on education is especially important. The perceived success of the army programme was used to present intelligence as the most important measure of human ability, which could be used successfully to categorise pupils and predict their future performance in school. In the 1920s, Yerkes and Terman created the 'National Intelligence Tests' aimed at primary schoolchildren, arguing that 'the limits of a child's educability can be fairly accurately predicted by means of mental tests given in the first school year' (cited in Murdoch, 2007, p. 93). Similarly, intelligence testing became the basis of college recruitment. The Scholastic Aptitude Test, the standard college admissions exam in the United States, first introduced in 1926, was also broadly based on Yerkes's army intelligence tests (Murdoch, 2007).

This influence on educational policy extended beyond the borders of the United States. Intelligence testers had important followers in Britain. In 1938, Sir Cyril Burt, an influential figure in British education at the time, argued, just like Yerkes and Terman had done 15 years earlier, that a child's intellectual development is governed by a 'single general factor, usually known as "general intelligence"' and therefore that intelligence testing at an early age could be used for educational selection (Burt, cited in Richardson, 1998, p. 109). This way of thinking underpinned the subsequent development of the 11-plus exam.

You read about the 11-plus exam in Chapter 1 of *Investigating Intelligence*.

However, the legacy of the army mental tests extends beyond the popularisation of mass intelligence testing in educational or commercial contexts. Yerkes's research had a deeper political dimension which brought the soundness and relevance of mental testing into question. It is to this aspect of the army testing programme that we turn in Section 3.

Summary

- During the First World War, Robert Yerkes and his team developed a test of intelligence for the purpose of screening US Army recruits.

- Yerkes's intelligence test contained two versions: the Alpha test, aimed at recruits who could read and speak English; and the Beta test, which was given to illiterate recruits or those who did not have a good command of the English language.

- The army testing programme signalled the beginning of mass testing of intelligence for purposes of screening and selection that is still used today in schools and in job recruitment around the world.

3 Interpreting the findings of the army tests

Once the testing of army recruits ended in 1918, Yerkes found himself in possession of data on the mental abilities of 1.7 million men. He believed that this massive amount of information could be used to draw meaningful inferences about the nature of intelligence, and about what causes individual differences in intellectual ability. The conclusions which Yerkes drew, however, were highly problematic.

3.1 Yerkes's (mis)reading of the results

You learned about test norms in Chapter 1, Section 2.3, of *Investigating Intelligence.*

Having analysed the results of the army testing programme, Yerkes (1921) drew two broad conclusions. First, that the average intelligence of the population of the United States was lower than previously thought. When compared with a set of test norms that had been developed by Terman, the recruits performed very poorly. The average American soldier appeared to perform similarly to what was expected of a 13-year-old child. Yerkes's second conclusion was as contentious. He argued that the performance on the tests revealed a clear hierarchy among social groups: the wealthy were more intelligent than the poor, white people were more intelligent than African-Americans, and when it came to immigrants, people originating from Northern and Western Europe were more intelligent than the Slavs and Jews of Eastern Europe, or the people of Southern Europe.

Eugenics movement
A movement that advocated the improvement of human genetic traits through the promotion of reproduction of people with desired traits and limiting reproduction of people with undesirable traits.

There was very little in Yerkes's controversial conclusions that had not been said before. In Chapter 1 you read that as early as the mid nineteenth century, Francis Galton and the craniometrists compared people of different class or racial background, drawing conclusions that reinforced the political prejudices of that era and upheld social hierarchies. They also believed that intelligence is innate, and therefore fixed and unchangeable. This kind of thinking continued to dominate intelligence research in the first half of the twentieth century, and it guided Yerkes's interpretation of the results. At this time, intelligence measurement was especially popular among exponents of the **eugenics movement** (Gould, 1996). The eugenicists not only believed that there are innate differences in ability between groups in society, but they also advocated the promotion of reproduction among people thought to be worthy and 'superior', while seeking to limit the reproduction of those believed to be 'inferior'. The principles of eugenics were reflected in both of Yerkes's conclusions. He, like many before him, allowed political prejudice and misguided convictions to drive the interpretation of scientific data.

What makes Yerkes's conclusions especially surprising is that the actual pattern of results from the army tests lends itself to a very different, and arguably much more obvious, interpretation (Gould, 1996; Murdoch, 2007). For example, as Yerkes (1921) himself pointed out, the study revealed the following about the performance of US Army recruits:

- There was a strong link between the score on the army tests and the amount of schooling a person had received. The longer someone attended school, the better the performance on the test.

- Diseases associated with poverty, such as hookworm infection, were more likely to be found among individuals who scored poorly on the army tests.

- Among recruits who came from immigrant communities, there was a strong relationship between the test score and the number of years they had spent in the United States before they took the test.

Activity 2.2

What conclusions about the origins of the differences in intelligence would you draw from these findings? Do you think that they support the conclusions Yerkes drew from the study?

The first finding points to the possibility that the army tests were in fact *not* assessing some underlying, and innate, intellectual ability independent of experience or education. Rather, they assessed the kind of knowledge and skills that people acquire through schooling. This is why recruits who had attended school longer did better on the tests. Similarly, the second finding – that there is a link between poverty and scores on the tests – suggests that environmental conditions such as material deprivation, poverty and poor health provision influenced the development of the kind of abilities assessed by the tests. Given that, at the time, poverty was closely associated with poor schooling, this once again suggested that 'intelligence', as measured by the army tests, was linked to education. Finally, the third finding opens up the possibility that performance on both Alpha and Beta tests depended not so much on innate ability, as Yerkes had assumed, but on the familiarity with the English language and American culture and way of life.

Taken together, these findings suggest that the army tests contained a significant cultural and class bias. They disadvantaged the poor and the underprivileged, which at the time included a large proportion of the African-American community, as well as immigrants. This is somewhat obvious when one looks at the content of the Alpha test (see Table 2.1): performance on many of the subtests required knowledge of American culture and history, a good command of the English language, and other competencies that are usually obtained in school.

Similarly, contrary to Yerkes's intentions, the Beta test did not create a level playing field for the illiterate and those who did not speak English well. The illiterate recruits, many of whom had never been to school, still needed to use a pen, write down numbers and symbols, and understand the demands of a testing situation. Knowledge of English may have been irrelevant to the Beta tasks themselves but not to understanding instructions about what was required. Also, in the picture completion tasks some of the items were likely to be more familiar to individuals from a certain class and cultural background: they included images of bowling and tennis, for example (see Figure 2.4). This affected recruits from a poor background, but also those from ethnic groups that had only recently started settling in the United States. Among them were Jews and other Eastern Europeans, which explains how they ended up near the bottom of Yerkes's hierarchy of nationalities.

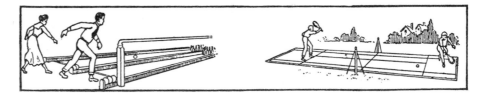

Figure 2.4 Cultural bias in the army mental tests: examples from the Beta test. The missing features are the bowling ball and the tennis net

(Source: Gould, 1996, p.241)

Yet, in drawing his conclusions, Yerkes chose to ignore the more logical and convincing interpretation of the evidence, and instead used his study to give an unwarranted aura of scientific credibility to the racist, anti-immigrant rhetoric which was widely espoused at the time. This, regrettably, is where his research had the greatest public impact. Shortly after the findings of the army studies were published, they were used to justify the quota on immigration from certain parts of Eastern and Southern Europe which was passed by the US Congress in 1924. According to Gould (1996, p. 262), this change in policy marked 'one of the greatest victories of **scientific racism** in American history', which Yerkes and his colleagues helped to bring about.

3.2   Lessons from the army testing programme

Let us pause for a moment now and consider the implications of the army testing programme and the way in which the results were interpreted.

Scientific racism
The manipulation of scientific theories and methods to justify the belief in racial superiority or inferiority.

Activity 2.3

Were you surprised by the involvement of some psychologists with the eugenics movement, and their contribution to the cause of scientific racism? Did you expect psychologists to be so heavily influenced by politics, and in particular by politics that promoted inequality, discrimination and racism?

Reading about the early intelligence research is always difficult for psychologists because it requires them to face one of the gloomiest episodes in the history of their discipline. However, awareness of the darker side of intelligence research is important for two reasons. First, it alerts us to the potential problems with interpreting performance on intelligence tests, especially in terms of cultural and class bias. This is a topic that we will return to in Chapter 3. Second, scientific racism, of the kind manifested in the interpretation of the results of the army testing programme, is not just of historical interest. Claims about certain ethnic and racial groups possessing inferior intelligence still circulate in society, and are often found in the propaganda of far-right movements (William and Law, 2012). Moreover, far-right movements have been helped in their project by some misinformed and discredited interpretations of psychological research, including *The Bell Curve* which you read about in Section 1. Such works continue to attribute differences in performance on a set of tests to differences in innate ability, rather than to differences in education, experience or opportunities, or the biased nature of the tests. The history of intelligence research provides a powerful reminder of *why* it is important to debunk this kind of bad science, which still raises its ugly head every now and then.

At the same time, it is important to note that the mainstream of psychological research has, in the light of strong scientific evidence, overwhelmingly rejected the notion that there are innate differences in intelligence between racial or ethnic groups. A recent overview of the relevant literature concluded that any apparent *group* differences in average performance on IQ tests 'are entirely due to environmental factors' (Nisbett et al., 2012, p. 146). These include differences in educational opportunity and socio-economic status, which are in large part a consequence of the long history of inequality and discrimination. One piece of evidence for this is the finding that the difference in the average performance on IQ tests between African-Americans and white Americans has narrowed substantially between 1972 and 2002, a period which saw a marked improvement in the quality of education, employment prospects and socio-economic status of the African-American community (Dickens and Flynn, 2006).

Moreover, you may be reassured to know that in the history of psychology as a whole there are far more examples where psychologists have found themselves on the correct side of the argument about human rights, equality and social justice. Since the Second World War in particular, there has been a substantial body of work in psychology which has looked at issues such as discrimination and prejudice. Later in the module you will learn about a number of studies that have sought to understand the psychology of fascism, the processes underpinning obedience to authority, and the development of aggression. These studies, unlike some of the early intelligence research, have helped bring about positive social change, and have promoted a fairer and more tolerant and inclusive society.

This research is introduced in Part 1 of the book *Investigating Psychology*.

3.3   Responses to the limitations of the army mental tests

The limitations of the early intelligence research, and in particular the class and cultural bias exposed by the failings of the army testing programme, have led to important changes in the way in which psychologists go about designing intelligence tests. One example is the stronger emphasis on robust standardisation procedures.

You will remember from Chapter 1, Secion 2.3 that standardisation is the process of establishing a set of test norms which are then used for the interpretation of test results. Standardisation involves administering the test to a sample of the population for which it is intended. By using large and representative standardisation samples, researchers can ensure that their test norms take into account, as far as it is possible, the cultural and social diversity of the population.

Thus, the more recent versions of the Wechsler Adult Intelligence Scale (WAIS) created for use in the United States have been standardised on samples which included thousands of people of different ethnicity, gender, educational level and geographical region (Aiken and Groth-Marnat, 2006). By comparison, when Wechsler created the first version of the scale in 1939, he standardised it on a sample of white, educated, employed adults from a middle-class, white-majority suburb of New York (Boake, 2002). An even more dramatic example of poor standardisation is the development of the adult version of the Stanford–Binet test undertaken by Terman in 1916. Norms about what constituted 'normal adult intelligence' were based on the performance of just 62 adults: 30 'business men' and 32 'high-school pupils' (Terman, 1916, p. 55). These were the norms that Yerkes used when he pronounced that the average US Army recruit's performance was similar to that of a 13-year-old child.

However, standardisation, no matter how rigorous, cannot fully remove the limitations of intelligence tests. Many practising psychologists – clinical, educational, forensic – who administer intelligence tests on a daily basis are mindful of this. Awareness of the extent to which cultural differences, or class and educational background can influence performance on IQ tests is especially important in societies like the UK, which are multicultural and attract a steady flow of immigrants from different countries of the world. In fact, there are certain parts of the UK, such as the city of Glasgow, where, because of particularly high cultural and social diversity, psychologists no longer use intelligence tests to assess the abilities of children. This is because they are not confident that intelligence tests can meaningfully identify the children's specific educational needs.

In the film *The limitations of intelligence tests*, which is available on the module website, you will see psychologists discuss the problem of cultural and class bias in intelligence testing. This issue is also considered in more detail in Chapter 3 of *Investigating Intelligence*.

Figure 2.5   How relevant are intelligence tests in a culturally and socially diverse society?

Summary

- The army testing programme has been criticised for both the way in which the tests were designed and how the results were interpreted.

- The Alpha and Beta tests revealed a significant class and cultural bias that disadvantaged African-American recruits, the poor, and recent immigrants.

- Yerkes's findings about the differences in intelligence between groups in society were driven by a political agenda and reflected prejudices espoused by the eugenics movement at the time.

- Psychologists today have overwhelmingly rejected the notion that there are innate differences in intelligence between ethnic and racial groups.

4   Genes and intelligence

Let us now turn to the other controversy surrounding intelligence which is also manifested in Yerkes's findings and which in many ways underpins the notion that groups differ in terms of intellectual ability. It is the assumption that intelligence has a strong genetic component. You will recall that Yerkes, and many of his contemporaries, not only believed that certain groups possess superior intelligence, but also that intelligence is innate, passed on through sexual reproduction. So, what exactly is the role of genetics in intelligence?

4.1   What is heritability?

At first sight there may not seem to be anything particularly remarkable about the claim that the kind of abilities assessed in an intelligence test is in part dependent on genes. For a start, people need a brain to act intelligently. The brain, just like the rest of the body, develops in part according to our **genetic code**. Also, a number of conditions that lead to lower performance on tests of intellectual ability (Down syndrome, for example) are known to be caused by genetic anomalies. This suggests that, at a very basic, organic level, genes do play a role in intelligence.

However, researchers interested in the role of genes in intelligence tend not to have been preoccupied with the question of *whether* intelligence has a genetic component. In much of intelligence research these days, it is generally accepted that differences in the genes that people carry account for some of the differences in intelligence (Neisser et al., 1996; Nisbett et al., 2012). Instead, the focus of research has been on establishing *how important* genes are, compared with environmental factors. This is known as the question of **heritability**. Heritability refers to the extent to which variability within a population, in a particular trait or characteristic (in this case intelligence), is explained by differences in genetic make-up.

The concept of heritability is difficult to get to grips with, and it is often misunderstood. There are two important things to keep in mind. First, estimates about the heritability of intelligence do not tell us anything about how much genes, or the environment, will affect the intelligence of a particular *individual* (Deary, 2001). Second, these estimates tell us nothing about the origin of the differences in

Genetic code
The rules which govern how information encoded within genetic material (the DNA) will be translated into proteins, the building blocks of any living organism.

Heritability
The extent to which differences in a trait, characteristic or ability within a population is due to genetic differences.

intelligence between groups (Gould, 1996). Let us look at each of these issues in turn.

Researchers looking at the heritability of IQ are keen to point out that any individual's intelligence will always be the product of a complex (and unpredictable) interaction between a genetic predisposition and environmental factors (Nisbett et al., 2012; Asbury and Plomin, 2013). This is a very different proposition to that once advanced by the likes of Galton, Yerkes or other eugenicists, whose work you read about in Sections 2 and 3. Their claim was that intelligence is innate, fixed by one's genetic heritage, and by and large unalterable by circumstances in life. They argued that genes *determine* intelligence.

By contrast, contemporary heritability studies recognise that both genes and the environment are important in the development of an *individual's* intelligence. The central focus of research has been, instead, to establish to what extent each of these factors accounts for differences in intelligence within a *population*. The key thing to remember, however, is that regardless of how heritable intelligence is found to be, it tells us only about the relative importance of genes *generally*, and nothing about the origins of any individual's abilities (Nisbett et al., 2012).

You will learn more about heritability in the online activity *Genes and intelligence.*

Also, just as heritability tells us nothing about how genetic make-up will influence the intelligence of a particular individual, it also tells us nothing about the origin of the differences in average intelligence *between groups*. As you read in Section 3, any differences in average performance on IQ tests that might exist between people of different racial backgrounds, for example, can be fully accounted for by environmental factors, such as differences in socio-economic status or educational opportunities. In fact, a common misunderstanding of heritability is that if genes account for some of the differences in IQ between *individuals*, they also must account for some of the apparent differences between *groups* (Gould, 1996). But this is not the case. Differences between individuals and differences between groups are two very different things: even if genes might account for some of the differences in IQ between individuals (regardless of their ethnic or racial origin), the differences between *groups* could still only reflect differences in environmental factors, such as cultural background, or the comparative disadvantages experienced by minority populations.

4.2 Evidence of heritability

Today, when the **human genome** – the complete set of genetic information contained in the human DNA – has been successfully mapped, there should be a way of directly addressing the question about the role of genes in intelligence. If intelligence is indeed partly inherited, it should be possible to identify a gene, or set of genes, that differentiates high performers on IQ tests from low performers. And yet, the quest for such genes has yielded no result (Deary et al., 2010). Our understanding of intelligence suffers from what Robert Plomin (2013), one of the leading researchers in this area, called the 'missing heritability problem'.

Note, however, the choice of term used here: the genes are said to be 'missing' rather than 'non-existent'. The assumption is that there *is* a genetic infrastructure behind some of the differences in intelligence, but that it remains hidden. So how do psychologists go about investigating the heritability of intelligence?

You might be surprised to hear that the concept of heritability originates from animal breeding programmes (Nisbett et al., 2012). For centuries, people have been interested in the extent to which certain desirable traits in animals (e.g. the amount of milk a cow produces, the quality of the wool on a sheep, agility in a horse) are passed on through genes. Such knowledge had practical application: traits found to be heritable could be maximised through controlled breeding.

In the case of animal research, estimates about the heritability of a trait are derived from carefully designed studies in which researchers control both breeding and aspects of the environment. By studying the effect of these manipulations of genes and the environment on a particular characteristic or trait, they draw conclusions about its heritability (Nisbett et al., 2012).

As you can imagine, similar research cannot be conducted on humans, for very good reasons. Psychologists (and all other scientists, including doctors, geneticists, molecular biologists, etc.) are governed by a strict code of **ethics**. Research ethics stipulate, among many other things, that research should not undermine the psychological well-being, physical health, personal values or dignity of those who participate in it. All of these would be violated if a researcher modelled an experiment on heritability in human participants on animal breeding programmes. So, when studying the heritability of human traits, researchers have to rely

Human genome
The complete set of genetic information contained in the human DNA.

Ethics
Principles that determine right and wrong conduct. In psychological research, ethics refers to the codes and principles that researchers should adhere to. You will learn about ethics in psychological research in Chapter 2 of *Investigating Psychology*.

on naturally occurring instances where it might be possible to distinguish the effects of genes from the effects of the environment on differences in intelligence.

One typical method of studying heritability involves twin studies. As you are probably aware, there are two types of twins: identical and non-identical. Identical twins, who have developed from the same fertilised egg (monozygotic twins), share 100 per cent of their genes. Non-identical twins, who have developed from two separate fertilised eggs (dizygotic twins), share 50 per cent of their genes (see Figure 2.6). In twin studies, researchers are looking at whether the similarity in intelligence between identical twins is greater than between non-identical twins. If identical twins (who share all of their genes) can be shown to be more similar to each other compared with non-identical twins (who share half of their genes), then this would suggest that intelligence has a genetic component (Asbury and Plomin, 2013).

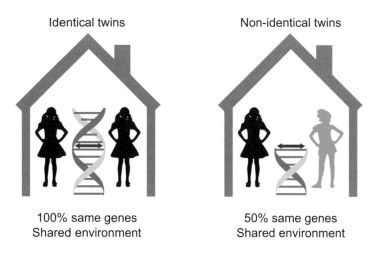

Identical twins   Non-identical twins

100% same genes   50% same genes
Shared environment   Shared environment

Figure 2.6   Twin studies: are identical twins more similar in intelligence to each other than non-identical twins?

Another method involves studying children who have been adopted. Adopted children share half of their genes with each of their biological parents, but they do not share an environment with them. At the same time, those same children share no genes with their adoptive parents, but they do share an environment (see Figure 2.7). By comparing the adopted children's intelligence with that of their biological and adoptive parents, psychologists have sought to estimate the relative importance of genes and the environment on intelligence. If the adopted children's IQ is more similar to that of their biological parents, even though they have been raised in a different family, this would indicate that genes play an important role in accounting for individual differences in intelligence. Conversely, if the adopted children's IQ is closer to that of the adoptive parents, with whom they do not share any genes, this would indicate that environment plays a more influential role.

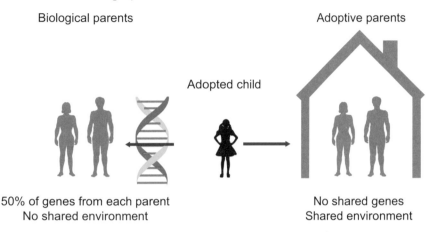

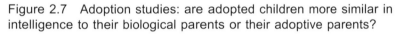

Figure 2.7   Adoption studies: are adopted children more similar in intelligence to their biological parents or their adoptive parents?

There is also a third method, which combines the basic principles of adoption and twin studies. It involves studying the rare cases where twins have been separated in early childhood and reared in different families. In studies of twins reared apart, what is of interest is whether the abilities of identical twins who grew up apart (who share their genes, but not the environment) are as similar as those of identical twins who grew up together (and therefore share both the genes and the environment; see Figure 2.8). If twins reared apart can be shown to be as similar to each other, in terms of IQ scores, as twins who grew up together, this would indicate that, when it comes to explaining differences in intelligence, genes are more important than the environment (Bouchard et al., 1990).

In all three types of heritability studies, researchers will use statistical procedures to generate a **heritability estimate**: a single figure, often expressed as a percentage, which describes to what extent variability in intelligence in the population is accounted for by variability in genes.

The results of heritability studies have tended to support the idea that differences in intelligence are, in part, due to genetic factors. In general, adopted children have been found to be more similar in intelligence to their biological parents than to their adoptive parents. Identical twins

Heritability estimate
An estimate of the extent to which variability in intelligence in the population is accounted for by variability in genes.

Identical twins raised together

Identical twins raised apart

100% same genes
Shared environment

100% same genes
Different environment

Figure 2.8   Twins raised apart studies: are identical twins raised apart as similar in intelligence to each other as identical twins raised together?

are, again generally, more similar to each other in terms of intelligence than non-identical twins. This similarity among identical twins is apparent even when they have been raised apart. Precise estimates about the relative importance of genes in relation to the environment vary, however. Some studies have argued that genes account for up to 80 per cent of variability in intelligence, and only around 20 per cent is due to the environment (Plomin and Thompson, 1993; Nisbett et al., 2012). Overall, studies tend to place the heritability estimate between 40 and 80 per cent (Deary, 2001).

4.3   Methodological critique of heritability studies

At first sight, the twin, adoption, and twins reared apart studies seem fairly straightforward and on relatively solid ground. There is a clear logic to each method, and given that direct experimentation with humans is impossible for ethical reasons, they appear to have made the most of circumstances in which the relative contribution of genes and the environment could be assessed. Nevertheless, a closer scrutiny of the research reveals a number of problems, all of which have one thing in common: they underestimate the role of environmental factors and exaggerate the role of genes.

Let us examine the twin studies approach first, given that this is the most commonly used method. Twin studies are based on the assumption that while identical and non-identical twins share different proportions of their genes (100 and 50 per cent, respectively), each pair of twins, regardless of whether they are identical or non-identical, will share roughly the same 'amount' and 'kind' of environment. In other words, a pair of twins, irrespective of how much of their genetic material they share (whether they are identical or non-identical), will live together in the same home, enjoy the same challenges and opportunities, and will be treated in the same way by their parents and other people around them. This is what is known as the **equal environment assumption**.

However, there is a fundamental problem with this assumption. The experiences of identical and non-identical twins, in terms of how much of their environment they share, have been shown to be very different (Joseph and Ratner, 2013). Identical twins tend to experience much more similar environments than non-identical twins, for no other reason than that they are *seen* as identical by others. They are more likely to resemble each other physically, which means that they will tend also to be treated as more similar by people around them: identical twins are more likely to be dressed alike or to share a bedroom, for example (Richardson, 1998).

This is an important point because some of the observed differences between identical and non-identical twins, in terms of how similar their IQs are, may not be due to the greater proportion of shared genes, as heritability studies assume. They might in fact be due to the environment, that is, to the fact that identical twins, as well as sharing more genes, also undergo much more similar experiences than non-identical twins (Joseph and Ratner, 2013).

Similar methodological problems are to be found in the twins reared apart studies. The central assumption behind this method is that twins who were reared apart were raised in *different* environments. This, after all, is what researchers argue enables them to separate out environmental influences from genetic ones: separated identical twins are assumed to share *all* of their genes but *none* of the environment. Hence the observed similarity between separated twins is attributed to common genetic heritage, but not to the environment.

And yet, many of the twins included in these studies shared quite a lot of their environment. First, they spent some of their childhood together. Children are rarely adopted at birth and this means that many of the twins had lived together for a number of years before separation, sometimes for as long as eleven years (Pedersen et al., 1992). Therefore, they shared the environment and experiences during key periods of psychological development. This makes separating out the relative

Equal environment assumption
The assumption in twin studies that twin pairs raised together experience roughly equal environments.

influence of 'nature' and 'nurture' on IQ much less straightforward (Richardson, 1998).

Furthermore, even after separation many of the twins were raised in a similar environment. Some of them were not adopted through welfare organisations or social services but were simply raised in different branches of the same family, by a family friend, or a neighbour. Such 'informal' adoption arrangements meant that some of the children, while supposedly raised 'apart', grew up within the same community or neighbourhood, attended the same school, or even socialised occasionally (Bouchard et al., 1990). These issues have led a group of critics to suggest that 'the technical use of the word "separated"' by scientists running the twins reared apart studies 'differs from the usage of the same word by ordinary people' (Rose et al., 1984, p. 108).

Another criticism, which applies to all three methods used in heritability studies, is the way in which researchers define 'environment' (Richardson, 1998). In Chapter 1, you read that many aspects of environmental and cultural experience – parental involvement in learning, educational provision, a supportive environment that promotes self-confidence and motivation, etc. – are important predictors of IQ scores. However, when assessing the relative importance of genes and environment, heritability studies tend to look only at a limited range of environmental factors. For example, one influential study of twins reared apart considered things like the availability of 'household facilities' – such as an 'unabridged dictionary' or a 'telescope' – and used this as a measure of 'cultural and intellectual resources' in the home (Bouchard et al., 1990, p. 225). These crude measures of 'environment' tell us nothing about how the 'resources' were used, just as it remains unclear why having a telescope, for example, would enhance the kind of intellectual abilities measured in IQ tests.

All of these methodological limitations of heritability studies tend to result in some of the variability in IQ which is due to environmental influences being apportioned to genes, thus inflating the estimates about the heritability of intelligence. Given how heritability studies define 'environment' and what constitutes an 'equal' or 'different' environment, it is perhaps unsurprising that they have so often concluded that 'nurture' does not account for the variability in intelligence as much as 'nature'.

Figure 2.9 Promotion of self-confidence and motivation: an environmental factor linked to performance on IQ tests

4.4 Why is heritability important?

The limitations of the current research on heritability go beyond the methodological issues which we have just looked at. In recent years, a number of psychologists and geneticists have argued that research in this area needs to move beyond trying to calculate the extent to which either genes or environment explain the variability in human characteristics, including IQ. This is because the two factors – genes and environment – are so deeply intertwined that their individual contributions are not only impossible to disentangle; they are also irrelevant. As Turkheimer (2011) explains, it is inevitable that genes and the environment both contribute to the development of human characteristics. But they do so by feeding into a mechanism – a developing human being living in the world – that is so complex that the individual contributions of either specific genes or specific aspects of the environment become lost. Therefore, research needs to move beyond estimates of heritability and begin to look at *interactions* between genes and environment. However, according to Turkheimer (2011), doing so lies beyond the current understanding of human genetics, and requires new, yet to be developed ways of studying the origins of complex human characteristics.

And yet, in spite of these calls for a new way of thinking about genes and the environment, heritability studies continue to be carried out around the world. This invites a number of questions. If researchers themselves admit that putting a figure on the heritability of intelligence 'makes no sense' because genes and the environment always interact in infinitely complex ways (Nisbett et al., 2012, p. 132), then why are these studies deemed so important? Why does heritability matter?

One possible reason is that it has been hoped that heritability would help overcome the fundamental problem of the psychology of intelligence, namely that we actually know very little about what intelligence, as measured by IQ tests, actually is. By now you will be aware that, in the context of intelligence testing, our understanding of the concept of intelligence comes not from *direct* observation and measurement, but exclusively from analyses of correlations between performance on different tasks. In other words, we *infer* how human intellectual abilities are organised from the results of the tests. The findings that intellectual abilities measured by IQ tests are, in part, passed through the genes, offer comfort that intelligence is in some sense 'real', at least as real as other measurable, and heritable, human characteristics, such as height, shoe size or short-sightedness.

The issue that intelligence cannot be observed directly but must be inferred from performance was covered in Chapter 1, Section 4.

Summary

- Heritability of intelligence refers to the extent to which differences in IQ within a population are explained by differences in genetic make-up. Estimates of the relative importance of genes are called heritability estimates.

- Heritability studies use naturally occurring instances where it might be possible to distinguish the effects of genes from the effects of the environment. These include twin studies, adoption studies and studies of twins who have been reared apart.

- A number of methodological problems associated with heritability studies have been identified. Most of these have led to the role of genes being overestimated.

- Recent research suggests that rather than trying to estimate the relative importance of genes and the environment, the focus of research should shift towards examining how genes and the environment interact to produce complex human characteristics, such as intelligence.

5 Conclusion

In this chapter, we examined two claims about intelligence that have caused particular controversy over the years. First, the claim that there are innate differences in intelligence between groups in society, and second, that differences in IQ between individuals have an important genetic basis. As we have seen, both of these claims have been challenged in different ways. The flawed conclusion about group differences in intelligence that Yerkes drew from the mass testing of army recruits was used for many years to prop up and maintain the marginalisation and oppression of those already disenfranchised. Subsequent re-examination of his findings supported a very different set of conclusions: the cultural bias built into the tests exposed the overwhelming importance of environmental influences (such as education, familiarity with American culture and way of life, etc.) on performance.

The second claim, that there is an important genetic basis to intelligence, has been underpinned by heritability studies which have variously estimated that genes account for between 40 and 80 per cent of differences in IQ. This claim is less inherently controversial, in that there is broad agreement that genes will have *some* influence on intelligence. However, as we have seen, one line of criticism has focused on the methods used in heritability research, arguing that twin and adoption studies overestimate the influence of genes precisely because they under-appreciate the complex diversity of environmental influences. Heritability research has also been challenged for assuming that the role of genes and the environment can be meaningfully disentangled. A more productive line of enquiry, it is suggested, would be to explore the interaction of genes and environment and what influence this has on the development of human intelligence.

You may have noticed that in the case of both group differences and heritability, the debates have focused on the interpretation of evidence. Yerkes, for instance, did indeed collect evidence for his argument but, as you have seen, evidence can be fallible if research is poorly designed or misinterpreted. Consequently, being a psychologist, and a scientist, involves *evaluating* evidence and the conclusions that are drawn from psychological research. This includes scrutinising, and criticising, the work of other psychologists, differentiating strong evidence from weak evidence, pointing out methodological shortcomings, and identifying, where possible, alternative and more plausible interpretations of the findings.

In Chapter 3, we will continue our critical look at the study of intelligence by exploring some of the alternative ways of thinking about what intelligence is and how it can be assessed, and what might be the implications of this for the way we think about human abilities in the real world.

References

Aiken, L. R. and Groth-Marnat, G. (2006) *Psychological Testing and Assessment*, 12th edn, Boston, MA, Pearson.

Asbury, K. and Plomin, R. (2013) *G is for Genes: The Impact of Genetics on Education and Achievement*, Chichester, John Wiley & Sons.

Boake, C. (2002) 'From the Binet–Simon to the Wechsler–Bellevue: tracing the history of intelligence testing', *Journal of Clinical and Experimental Neuropsychology*, vol. 24, no. 3, pp. 383–405.

Bouchard, T. J., Lykken, D. T., McGue, M., Segal, N. L. and Tellegen, A. (1990) 'Sources of human psychological differences: the Minnesota study of twins reared apart', *Science*, vol. 250, no. 4978, pp. 223–8.

Deary, I. J. (2001) *Intelligence: A Very Short Introduction*, Oxford, Oxford University Press.

Deary, I. J., Penke, L. and Johnson, W. (2010) 'The neuroscience of human intelligence differences', *Nature Reviews: Neuroscience*, vol. 11, pp. 201–11.

Dickens, W. T. and Flynn, J. R. (2006) 'Black Americans reduce the racial IQ gap: evidence from standardization samples', *Psychological Science*, vol. 17, pp. 913–20.

Gould, S. J. (1996) *The Mismeasure of Man*, Revised and Expanded Edition, London, Penguin.

Herrnstein, R. J. and Murray, C. (1994) *The Bell Curve: Intelligence and Class Structure in American Life*, New York, The Free Press.

Joseph, J. and Ratner, C. (2013) 'The fruitless search for genes in psychiatry and psychology: time to re-examine a paradigm', in Krimsky, S. and Gruber, J. (eds) *Genetic Explanations: Sense and Nonsense*, Cambridge, MA, Harvard University Press, pp. 94–106.

Murdoch, S. (2007) *IQ: A Smart History of a Failed Idea*, Hoboken, NJ, John Wiley & Sons.

Neisser, U., Boodoo, G., Bouchard, T. J., Jr., Boykin, A. W., Brody, N., Ceci, S. J., Halpern, D. F., Loehlin, J. C., Perloff, R., Sternberg, R. J. and Urbina, S. (1996) 'Intelligence: knowns and unknowns', *American Psychologist*, vol. 51, pp. 77–101.

Nisbett, R. E., Aronson, J., Blair, C., Dickens, W., Flynn, J., Halpern, D. F and Turkheimer, E. (2012) 'Intelligence: new findings and theoretical developments', *American Psychologist*, vol. 67, no. 2, pp. 130–59.

Pedersen, N. L., Plomin, R., Nesselroade, J. R. and McClearn, G. E. (1992) 'A quantitative genetic analysis of cognitive abilities during second half of the life span', *Psychological Science*, vol. 3, pp. 346–53.

Plomin, R. (2013) 'Child development and molecular genetics: 14 years later', *Child Development*, vol. 84, no. 1, pp. 104–20.

Plomin, R. and Thompson, L. A. (1993) 'Genetics and high cognitive ability', in Bock, G. R. and Ackrill, K. (eds) *CIBA Foundation Symposium 178: The Origins and Development of High Ability*, Chichester, John Wiley & Sons.

Richardson, K. (1998) *The Origins of Human Potential: Evolution, Development and Psychology*, London, Routledge.

Rose, S., Kamin, L. J. and Lewontin, R. C. (1984) *Not in Our Genes*, Harmondsworth, Penguin.

Terman, L. (1916) *The Measurement of Intelligence*, Boston, MA, Houghton Mifflin Company.

Turkheimer, E. (2011) 'Commentary: variation and causation in the environment and genome', *International Journal of Epidemiology*, vol. 40, pp. 598–601.

William, S. and Law, I. (2012) 'Legitimising racism: an exploration of the challenges posed by the use of indigeneity discourses by the far right', *Sociological Research Online*, vol. 17, no. 2 [Online]. Available at www.socresonline.org.uk/17/2/2.html (Accessed 29 November 2013).

Yerkes, R. M. (1921) 'Psychological examining in the United States Army', *Memoirs of the National Academy of Sciences*, vol. 15, parts 1–3, Washington, D. C., Government Printing Office.

Yoakum, C. and Yerkes, R. M. (1920) *Army Mental Tests*, New York, NY, Henry Holt and Company.

Chapter 3
Beyond the IQ

Contents

Aims and objectives

After studying this chapter you should be able to:

- discuss some of the challenges in constructing a culturally neutral intelligence test
- appreciate the difficulties of determining what it is that intelligence tests actually measure
- describe the role of IQ measurement in the diagnosis of learning disability and identify some of the criticisms of current diagnostic criteria
- outline the concept of emotional intelligence and how it differs from traditional notions of intelligence.

1   Introduction

In the first two chapters of this book, we examined two important issues regarding intelligence: we looked at how intelligence is measured (Chapter 1), and at how one might account for differences in intelligence (Chapter 2). In doing so, we examined some of the landmark developments in this area of psychological research and engaged with a number of contentious issues about intelligence, including the questions of heritability, group differences, and cultural and class bias in IQ tests.

In this concluding chapter, we will explore how psychology might think about intelligence in a different way, by moving away from the idea of IQ as a measure of human ability, and why it may be useful for it do so. We will be looking at three specific, and related, issues. First, whether it is possible to create a test of intelligence that is free of cultural and class bias, one that would effectively eliminate the kind of shortcomings that Roberts Yerkes's army testing programme exposed so dramatically. As we will see, this is not just an important technical issue about test design, but one that cuts to the heart of what intelligence actually *is*.

Second, we will examine a specific contemporary context where intelligence measurement affects human lives in profound ways: the diagnosis of learning disability. Intelligence measurement is enshrined in the official definition of learning disability, and IQ testing is routinely used to determine whether or not a person has a learning disability. We will consider the merits of this longstanding diagnostic practice, and reflect on some recent proposals for alternative ways of defining learning disability.

Third, we will look briefly beyond the notion of IQ and examine a different aspect of human abilities, and intelligence, which has captured the imagination of psychologists and the general public over the last quarter of a century: *emotional intelligence*. Advocates of emotional intelligence argue that the capacity to engage with emotions, one's own and those of others, is an important ability, one that may be much more relevant to achieving success at school and in the workplace than IQ. We will look at what emotional intelligence is, how it is measured, and to what extent it offers a useful alternative to the traditional conceptualisation of mental abilities.

Summary

- One of the current developments in the study of intelligence involves moving beyond IQ to think about intellectual abilities in different ways.

- Three key areas being explored in this chapter are the development of culture-free intelligence tests, the role of intelligence measurement in the diagnosis of learning disability, and the concept of emotional intelligence.

2 Intelligence: a measure of 'strength' or 'distance'?

In Chapter 2, you read that one way in which psychologists have sought to resolve the issue of class and cultural bias in intelligence measurement is by seeking to create more sophisticated, standardised tests. Eliminating bias is a central goal in intelligence research because a key assumption behind the concept of intelligence is that it involves an aspect of human intellectual functioning that is universal and independent of differences in culture, lifestyle, wealth or educational experience.

In contemporary discussions about biases in intelligence testing, one test in particular is often highlighted as a good example of an intelligence measure unaffected by things like acquired knowledge, schooling or previous experience. It is the Raven's Progressive Matrices test. Unlike most other IQ tests, Raven's Progressive Matrices test includes no words, and therefore does not require reading ability, nor does it have any pictures of concrete objects that may be more familiar to people from one culture than others. This is why the test is frequently used in the assessment of fluid intelligence, which includes abilities such as logical thinking and problem solving independent of acquired knowledge. More importantly, tasks similar to those featured in the Raven's Progressive Matrices test have been incorporated in other popular intelligence tests, such as the Wechsler Adult Intelligence Scale (WAIS). In the WAIS, these tasks form the 'matrix reasoning' subtest, which assesses non-verbal, perceptual reasoning.

2.1 Towards a culture-free test: Raven's Progressive Matrices

The Raven's Progressive Matrices test was first developed in the 1930s by the British psychologist John C. Raven. Raven sought to create a test of human intelligence that would be much simpler and quicker to administer than the then dominant Stanford–Binet scale. His motivations were not dissimilar to those behind the development of Yerkes's Beta test, which you read about in Chapter 2. Not only was Raven interested in developing a quick and easy test suitable for mass application in schools or the workplace, he was also interested in one that could be used to assess people who have a poor command of the

The concept of fluid intelligence, proposed by Raymond Cattell in the 1970s, was introduced in Chapter 1, Section 4.2, of *Investigating Intelligence*.

You learned about the Wechsler Adult Intelligence Scale in Chapter 1, Section 4.1, of *Investigating Intelligence*. Perceptual reasoning was introduced there as one of the core components of general intelligence as measured by the WAIS-IV.

English language, or whose poor level of schooling made tests of verbal ability inappropriate (Raven, 1960).

There are currently three different versions of the Raven's Progressive Matrices test: the Standard version, designed for the general population; the Advanced version, which contains more complex items and is intended for those who do very well on the Standard test; and a third simplified test, the Coloured Matrices version; which is aimed at children and people who may have a learning disability. In this section, we will focus on the Standard test, although the basic principles behind the Raven's Progressive Matrices are shared by all three versions.

You read about the intellectual ownership of intelligence tests in Chapter 1, Box 1.1, of *Investigating Intelligence.*

The Standard Raven's Progressive Matrices test (the most recent version of which was published in the late 1990s) consists of 60 so-called 'matrix problems', that is, a series of shapes or patterns that form a 'design' which has a piece missing (Raven et al., 1998). Figure 3.1 shows an example of the kind of task involved in a matrix test. Because the test is protected by copyright, the example below is one that resembles one of Raven's Progressive Matrices rather than an actual 'matrix problem' used in the test.

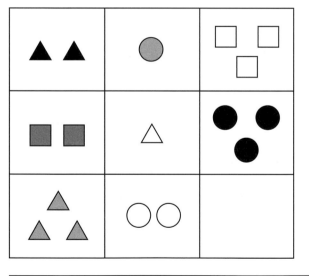

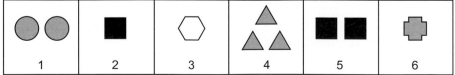

Figure 3.1   An example of a matrix problem similar to those found in the Raven's Progressive Matrices test

In the test, the task is to select, from a series of numbered alternatives, the missing piece that completes the matrix. The essence of the problem is to work out the rule, or set of rules, that governs the order and position of items within the matrix and use this to select the correct answer.

In the example presented in Figure 3.1, the correct answer is option 2. There are four things that need to be taken into account when solving this particular puzzle: the shapes (triangle, circle or square), the number of objects in each position within the matrix (one, two or three) the colour (white, black or grey) and, finally, how these different elements are arranged across rows and columns. As you may have spotted, each position within a row contains a different shape, a different colour and a different number of shapes. So, given that the first two positions in the bottom row contain three grey triangles and two white circles, a single black square is the only solution that completes the matrix in a way that satisfies all the rules.

Just like in other intelligence tests, the matrices are presented in ascending order of difficulty: they become increasingly more complex as the test progresses. The main source of complexity is the increasing number of 'rules' across rows and columns that need to be identified and applied simultaneously in order to correctly identify the missing piece of the matrix. The test is usually completed using a pen and paper, and takes about 40 minutes.

The Raven's Progressive Matrices test has been judged a success in terms of its apparent cultural neutrality. At first sight, one can see why Raven's test is said to be culturally neutral. It only includes abstract shapes, and to solve the puzzle the person taking the test does not even need to be familiar with the shapes. All that is required is the application of 'pure' skills of logical and abstract reasoning to figure out which answer completes the matrix. But is this really so?

Activity 3.1

Take another look at Figure 3.1. From what you have read about intelligence testing in Chapters 1 and 2, would you say that the Raven's Progressive Matrices test assesses the ability to solve problems independently of educational level or acquired knowledge? Try to think of two or three ways in which the performance on the Raven's Progressive

Matrices test might be affected by cultural or class background, or indeed by the kind of life experiences that someone might have had.

How did you get on? One thing you may have thought of is that, regardless of the specific nature of the task, the Raven's Progressive Matrices test is still an intelligence *test*. Someone with experience of schooling, or any kind of formal assessment, is likely to find the testing situation more familiar, which would enable them to perform better. Similarly, pen-and-paper tasks are themselves 'cultural tools', and as such are dependent on experience. This is not just an issue of whether or not someone knows how to use a pen, but rather, the extent to which they are used to using them in the context of a test, something that is, again, likely to be linked to a level of literacy and education (Richardson, 1998).

There are further ways in which performance on Raven's Progressive Matrices test is influenced by cultural background. You may have noticed that in the example in Figure 3.1, the bottom-right piece of the matrix is missing. This is a standard feature of the test, because it assumes that people process material from top to bottom and from left to right, and therefore that the piece on the bottom right is the 'last' piece in the matrix (Richardson, 2002). However, this only applies to cultural contexts where people read from left to right, top to bottom, as they do in most Western countries. This is not the case among people who read from right to left (e.g. in Arabic or Hebrew), or where words are traditionally written in vertical columns and read from top to bottom, right to left (e.g. in Japan, China or Korea). In fact, a separate test that takes this into account has been created for use in Arabic-speaking countries, which is in itself an acknowledgement that Raven's Progressive Matrices are not as neutral as has been suggested (Abdel-Khalek and Raven, 2006).

Class is another important factor here. As you read in Chapter 1, performance on IQ tests, regardless of their specific nature, has been shown to be influenced by confidence and motivation. Both of these are closely related to class and status. Children from working-class families, or disadvantaged backgrounds, tend to have a lower belief in their intellectual abilities and a lower sense of control of events around them, compared with children from a wealthier, middle-class background (Ward, 2013). This makes them less likely to perform well in a testing situation, particularly when faced with unfamiliar or challenging problems, like those in a Raven's Progressive Matrices test.

Finally, even though the matrices comprise abstract shapes, which test designers argue are culturally neutral, what the person completing the test is supposed to do with them is not culturally neutral. This goes beyond the obvious point that the person taking the test must be able to understand *verbal* instructions about what they are supposed to do. Applying different rules to solve a Raven's matrix involves a similar kind of mental manipulation of information to that required when interpreting tables with rows and columns, or when reading from a spreadsheet, for example (Richardson, 2002), not to mention things like completing jigsaw puzzles, doing Sudoku, or engaging with other tasks that involve handling or manipulating objects and images and developing strategies for doing so effectively. Exposure to these activities will vary significantly both between cultures and among different social groups within a culture. For example, in many countries people who live and work in cities will have very different life experiences and encounter different challenges from those who live and work in a rural setting.

Figure 3.2   Doing jigsaw puzzles, completing Sudoku and interpreting timetables involve a similar kind of mental processing to the Raven's Progressive Matrices test

2.2   Intelligence as 'distance'

The example of the Raven's Progressive Matrices test opens up the possibility that, in spite of the attempts to overcome biases in testing, intelligence measurement cannot be meaningfully separated from culture and experience. This has led some psychologists to argue that the central question in psychological research on human intellectual abilities should not be about how to build better tests that might isolate the 'raw' intellectual power from the 'noise' of culture and experience. Instead, it should be about recognising that culture, experience and intellectual reasoning are deeply intertwined (Richardson, 1998; Sternberg et al., 2001). Intelligence is always embedded in a social and cultural context, and for that reason tests will contain features which will be more familiar to some sections of society or parts of the world's population than to others.

Consider the following example. Tests of IQ – including the Raven's Progressive Matrices test – claim to measure the ability to solve abstract problems and manipulate numbers or images in the head, as well as the ability to process information quickly. Why are *these* features of intellectual functioning particularly important? Moreover, are they *universally* relevant, as some of the assumptions about intelligence imply? According to Sternberg et al. (2001), abilities measured in an intelligence test are, in fact, neither universally relevant nor intrinsically important. There are parts of the world in which intelligence is understood quite differently. For example, a study conducted in Taiwan found that there – and this holds true in many other countries of the Far East – someone regarded as 'intelligent' possessed a number of characteristics traditionally ignored by intelligence tests developed in the West, such as being able to relate well to others, or being confident in one's own abilities while also being modest about them (Yang and Sternberg, 1997). In Kenya, the popular definition of an 'intelligent child' included whether they performed housework without having to be told what needs doing (Harkness et al., 1992). In various parts of Africa, speed of processing, a staple ingredient of all contemporary intelligence tests, is not regarded as the defining feature of intelligence. On the contrary, acting intelligently there involves thinking slowly about a problem before attempting to solve it (Wober, 1974).

Therefore, what psychologists in the West have traditionally taken to be features of general, human intelligence reflect culturally specific ways of thinking about what it means to be 'smart'. What is more, abilities that for the past century have been considered worthy of measuring – abstract reasoning, or the speed of processing, for example – reflect the values, attitudes, experiences and opportunities of people from a particular social and educational background. This is why intelligence testing inevitably privileges certain social groups and marginalises others and, in doing so, inadvertently helps to reproduce inequality in society (Richardson, 1998).

The argument that intellectual ability is deeply embedded in cultural and societal processes has profound implications for our understanding of intelligence. It invites us to rethink the usefulness of both intelligence as a concept and intelligence testing as a practice.

According to Ken Richardson (1998, 2002), a vocal critic of the established approaches to intelligence, the starting point for assessing what we mean by 'intelligence' involves abandoning the analogy which lies at the core of much of the current understanding of the term. (An analogy is when something that is difficult to understand or make sense of is explained by comparison with something familiar.) You will remember from Chapters 1 and 2 that ever since the middle of the nineteenth century and the days of Francis Galton, intelligence has been perceived as a measure of intellectual or mental 'strength', a kind of generic reasoning 'power' – the g – that varies between people and predicts success at school and in the workplace. This analogy with physical *strength* persists in much of the current literature on intelligence. It underpins the idea that mental strength, just like physical strength, can be measured independently of one's background or life circumstances, and that what counts as intellectual 'strength' is universal. For Richardson, this is a profoundly misleading analogy. Because IQ tests measure culturally specific thinking and reasoning, they assess familiarity with a set of cultural tools, rather than some context-free, universal intellectual power. For this reason, when talking about intelligence, a more appropriate analogy might be that of *distance*. What IQ tests assess is actually social and cultural *distance* from (or proximity to) the kind of culturally specific ways of interpreting and thinking about problems and problem solving that are enshrined in IQ tests, and which test creators have traditionally assumed underpin intelligence. The 'closer' someone matches the culturally valued abilities built into a test, the higher that person will score on the test.

You will learn more about analogies and how they are used in psychology in Chapter 7 of *Investigating Psychology*.

It is important to note that the conceptualisation of intelligence as a measure of distance does not imply that assessing abilities is itself a pointless endeavour, or that the concept of individual differences in ability is irrelevant. Rather it suggests that it is necessary to begin to recognise both the diversity of human abilities and the fact that they are inseparable from the specific cultural and social context that a person inhabits. This requires moving away from the narrow concept of intelligence and IQ measurement, as they exist at present, in favour of an emphasis on a wider range of practical and creative abilities and skills, how they develop, and how they can be enhanced. A single concept of intelligence, in the way that it exists now, can never successfully capture the varied ways in which people reason, solve problems, and engage with complex ideas or learn from experience in everyday contexts.

2.3   The future of intelligence debates

Despite the various limitations of IQ testing and the controversies that have plagued this area of research over the past century, intelligence is still widely regarded within psychology as a useful and relevant concept. While it may be recognised that IQ tests are not perfect instruments, they are nevertheless treated, by many psychologists, as reliable measures of a generic, and universal, intellectual ability. For example, Ian J. Deary, a leading supporter of the idea of intelligence and intelligence testing, has gone so far as to describe this area of rescarch as 'arguably among the best and most resilient success stories in all of scientific psychology' (Deary, 2003, p. 534). Similarly, a more recent review of intelligence research by a group of leading American psychologists concluded that 'the measurement of intelligence is one of psychology's greatest achievements', although the authors conceded that it was also one of its 'most controversial' (Nisbett et al., 2012, p. 131). However, the report went on to claim that while there is 'some merit' to the various criticisms directed at intelligence, they do not undermine the inherent usefulness of the concept. Evidently, a 100-year-long tradition of intelligence research and measurement cannot be easily relinquished.

It is likely that vociferous debates about intelligence and intelligence measurement will continue in the future. Such diversity of views and polarisation of opinion is not uncommon in psychology. Most areas of psychology comprise a mixture of competing theories, viewpoints, methods of enquiry, and conclusions about psychological phenomena. Disagreement is not of itself a bad thing. In fact, research will often be guided and advanced to very good effect by debates and clashes between competing positions. Nonetheless, as you have learned in Chapter 2, what makes intelligence somewhat different is that the nature of the subject matter, and its troubled history, mean that deliberations about scientific evidence and its interpretation will inevitably raise a set of broader moral and political questions about differences between people.

Let us now turn to the next topic of this chapter, and consider an everyday context where measuring intelligence has considerable practical implications. Both in the UK and throughout much of the world, the diagnosis of learning disability is based, in large part, on the assessment of a person's IQ. In Section 3 we will look more closely at this diagnostic practice, and continue to pursue the question of whether intelligence tests represent a valuable and relevant way of assessing human abilities.

Summary

- Raven's Progressive Matrices test is an example of the attempt to create a culturally neutral measure of intelligence.

- The cultural neutrality of the Raven's Progressive Matrices test has been questioned on the grounds that it contains class and cultural bias and that performance depends on such things as experience, confidence and motivation.

- An alternative idea to the traditional analogy of intelligence as mental strength is the notion of intelligence as distance from (or proximity to) the culturally valued notions of what counts as intelligence.

3   IQ and learning disability

In the UK around 1.2 million people are believed to have some form of learning disability (Emerson et al., 2012). This represents about 2 per cent of the total population of the country. **Learning disability** refers to any condition that significantly affects the way in which a person learns new information and skills, understands new or complex information, or is able to cope independently with the demands of everyday life (Department of Health, 2001).

Learning disability is a very broad term which covers a wide range of conditions and levels of impairment. An important thing to bear in mind is that the concept of learning disability is different from that of **learning difficulties**. While learning *disability* tends to be associated with a more general impairment in intellectual abilities, learning *difficulties* refer to specific problems – with reading, or understanding numbers, for example – which might act as a barrier to reaching certain educational or academic goals, but are not linked to general intellectual functioning.

Learning disability can be more or less severe, which is why terms such as 'mild', 'moderate', 'severe' and 'profound' are sometimes used. This is in recognition of the fact that some people who have a learning disability can live independently, communicate effectively and have a job, while others might have multiple learning disabilities and require full-time care and help with the most basic daily tasks such as eating or washing. Also, there are many different causes of learning disability, including genetic anomalies (such as Down syndrome), conditions such as autism or severe epilepsy, problems during birth which lead to brain damage, and illness or brain injury during childhood.

In spite of the fact that people who have a learning disability are not a uniform group and will differ greatly in terms of their specific needs and the cause of the disability, what they have in common is that they will require some level of support and sometimes the involvement of qualified professionals in their care. Also, in most instances, children with a learning disability will have special educational needs. This is why the diagnosis of learning disability is so important: it carries consequences for children or adults who are being assessed, and their families and carers. Based on the assessment of a person's abilities, important decisions are made about what support they, and their family, will have access to and what resources will be allocated to that person's

Learning disability
Significant impairment in the ability to learn new information and skills, understand new or complex information, or to cope independently with the demands of everyday life.

Learning difficulties
Specific problems with reading, or understanding numbers, for example, which can prevent someone from reaching certain educational or academic goals but arc not linked to general intellectual functioning.

education and ongoing care. There are also significant legal implications associated with the diagnosis, including whether someone can be held criminally responsible, appear as a witness at a trial, share custody of children, or make decisions about their own medical treatment or financial affairs. This, therefore, is one of those contexts where intelligence measurement has a profound effect on people's lives and well-being.

3.1   The diagnosis of learning disability

In the UK, the diagnosis of learning disability is based on three core criteria (Department of Health, 2001). A person is deemed to have a learning disability if:

- they show significant impairment of intellectual functioning
- they show significant impairment of the ability to adapt to their environment or interact with people around them
- these impairments occurred before adulthood.

The first criterion is of particular interest to us here because judgement about the level of intellectual impairment is made on the basis of IQ tests. In the UK, this is usually either the child or the adult version of the Wechsler intelligence scale, depending on the age of the person being assessed (Webb and Whitaker, 2012). Following assessment by a qualified professional, a person will be deemed to have a 'significant impairment of intellectual functioning' if their IQ is below 70, that is, if they scored 69 or less on the age-appropriate intelligence test (BPS, 2000). Similar criteria are used in most countries around the world.

It is not by accident that the 'significant impairment of intellectual functioning' is always listed as the first criterion for assessing learning disability. This is because it is generally believed that IQ, unlike other factors such as the ability to adapt to the environment or to function socially, can be measured precisely and objectively using standardised tests. Also, it used to be taken for granted that people who have a low IQ will automatically have an impaired ability to function socially and, therefore, that a test of intellectual abilities should be central, if not sufficient on its own, to the diagnosis of learning disability (BPS, 2000). However, in recent decades there has been a shift away from this position in recognition that ability to function independently is not always directly linked to IQ. This is why in 2000 the British

Psychological Society (BPS) recommended that the diagnosis of learning disability should also always involve an independent assessment of whether a person can take care of their basic needs by themselves, and how they function in their environment. This should involve observation of the person being assessed (often on more than one occasion) and also consultation with at least one parent, carer or friend (BPS, 2000).

Regardless of the increasing recognition of the importance of criteria other than IQ, the fact remains that, at present at least, intelligence is central to the diagnosis of learning disability. One could even argue that IQ remains crucial for determining whether someone will be classified as having a learning disability, while assessment of their social and adaptive needs is mainly used to determine the level of care and support needed (Webb and Whitaker, 2012).

3.2   Setting the threshold for learning disability diagnosis

One question posed by the criteria for learning disability is why has 70 been chosen as a threshold for diagnosis? What is it that someone who has an IQ of 75, for example, can do that someone with the score of 65 cannot? What is it about the level of performance below 70 that is so 'impaired' that it warrants a diagnosis of learning disability?

The answer to these questions is quite simple. There is nothing particularly remarkable about the score of 70. In fact, a study by Whitaker (2004) found that many people with an IQ below 70 can cope with life and look after themselves without significant help, just as some people with an IQ above the threshold need the support of specialist services.

The reason why 70 and not another score was chosen is linked to the concept of normal distribution and the bell-shaped curve that is used to represent the distribution of intelligence in the population (see Figure 3.3).

You learned about the normal distribution of intelligence in Chapter 1, Section 3.2, of *Investigating Intelligence*.

Activity 3.2

Take a closer look at the normal distribution graph in Figure 3.3, which you already encountered in Chapter 1. Identify the point which marks the threshold for learning disability. According to the bell curve, how many IQ points away from the average score is the threshold for learning disability? What percentage of the population would fall under the category of 'learning disabled'?

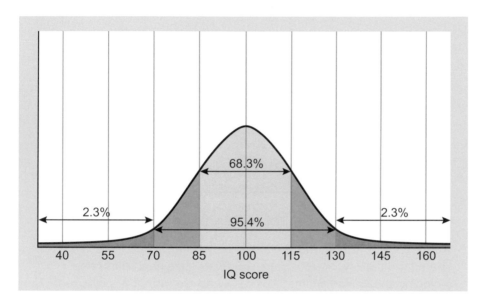

Figure 3.3   The 'bell curve': normal distribution of IQ

You will remember from Chapter 1 that intelligence tests are designed in such a way that the average IQ score is always 100, and approximately two-thirds of the population will register an IQ between 85 and 115, that is, within 15 points either side of the average (the light grey area in Figure 3.3). The score of 70 has been chosen as the threshold for the diagnosis of learning disability because it lies at twice that distance from the average, that is, 30 points below 100. In Figure 3.3, the area below 70 is shaded in dark grey, and the number above it indicates that approximately 2.3 per cent of the population would have some form of learning disability.

Now have a look at the corresponding area (also shaded in dark grey) on the right-hand side of the bell curve, where the high scores are. As you can see, according to the normal distribution curve, the same proportion of the population (just over 2 per cent) has an IQ above 130. This is the threshold used to determine whether someone can become a member of Mensa, an organisation that claims to be a 'society for bright people'. Mensa and similar associations are open only to those whose IQ score places them in the top 2 per cent of the population. Therefore, the definition of what it means to be 'bright', just like the definition of 'learning disability', is based on IQ scores, and expressed in *statistical terms*, that is, in terms of where a person is situated on the normal distribution curve, and how their score compares with other people's.

The score of 70 as a threshold for learning disability has a long history. Early intelligence researchers, including Goddard, Terman and Yerkes, whose work you read about in Chapter 2, used the same IQ score in the diagnosis of 'the feebleminded', the term used at the time to refer to people with learning disabilities (see Box 3.1). This continuity in the way in which learning disability is defined and assessed offers yet another example of the thread that runs through the history of intelligence research and binds current applications of IQ testing to the past.

Euphemism treadmill
The process whereby a word introduced to replace an offensive word over time itself becomes offensive, and is then replaced by another.

Box 3.1   The question of terminology

At the time of writing, the UK is the only country that uses the term 'learning disability'. In most other English-speaking countries, including the United States, Australia and Canada, the preferred term is 'intellectual disability'. The problem of terminology is further compounded by the fact that in the United States the term 'learning disability' is used to refer to what in the UK would be termed *learning difficulties* – specific impairments in reading, learning or processing information which are *not* linked to intelligence.

Over the past 150 years, there have been significant changes in the terminology used to refer to people who have a learning disability. People with varying levels of learning disability have been referred to, at different times, as *morons, cretins, idiots, imbeciles, feebleminded, retarded, mentally handicapped*, etc. The word *moron*, for example, was first used in the 1910s by the American psychologist Henry Goddard, whose work you encountered in Chapters 1 and 2. The term is derived from the Ancient Greek work *moros*, which means 'dull', and Goddard used it as a technical term to refer to people whose IQ was between 50 and 70. At the time, the word 'feebleminded' was a generic term used to refer to people with an IQ below 70, with 'morons' being the highest scoring group among the 'feebleminded'.

None of these words are used today, except as terms of abuse or ridicule. In fact, the terminology has changed several times as part of a process known as a **euphemism treadmill** (Pinker, 2003). This is when a word introduced to replace one that has become offensive itself acquires a pejorative meaning over time, and is then also replaced by another. Thus, the words 'feebleminded' or 'moron', which in the early twentieth century were used as technical terms, were eventually replaced by the word 'mentally retarded', until the word 'retard' became a term of insult, leading to a further change. It is therefore possible that over time, even words like 'learning disabled' or 'intellectually disabled', which many consider acceptable today, might acquire negative connotations, necessitating another change in official terminology.

The persistence of the euphemism treadmill in relation to words used to refer to disabilities, whether intellectual or physical, is important to think about because it serves as a powerful reminder of the long history of prejudice in society towards people with different forms of disability.

3.3 Problems with using IQ to diagnose learning disability

The various shortcomings of IQ tests, which are recognised by many practitioners, mean that in most contexts in which intelligence testing is used the overall IQ score is not actually the most important result. Psychologists often find the overall IQ score much less informative than the results on individual subtests. The subtests, in conjunction with other information about a person, can be used to make judgements about the *specific* things that they can and cannot do.

Furthermore, although most current intelligence tests will yield an overall IQ score, it is generally believed that this is only accurate within plus or minus 4 points (Webb and Whitaker, 2012). So, if someone is said to have scored, for example, 109 on an intelligence test, this means that it can be said with some confidence that their IQ lies somewhere between 105 and 113. The margin of error indicates that the score of 109 is not as precise as it might seem. And yet, when it comes to diagnosing learning disability, the single overall IQ score is the most important outcome of the test.

The limited value of the IQ score as a measure of intellectual ability was discussed in the film *Intelligence testing: practical applications*, which is available on the module website.

In his recent research, the British psychologist Simon Whitaker (2008) questioned the suitability of IQ tests as a diagnostic tool in the assessment of learning disability. Whitaker argues that intelligence tests, including the Wechsler scale, are in fact least accurate when assessing those at the lower IQ range, that is, people for whom testing will have

You read about test standardisation in Chapter 1, Section 2.3, of *Investigating Intelligence*.

the greatest practical consequence. Among people who do not perform well on an IQ test, the margin of error is much greater than 4 points, and can be as high as 13 points. One source of this greater margin of error is that low scorers tend to be more affected by the testing situation and by things like mood, stress, or rapport with the person administering the test (Whitaker, 2008). Another reason is that IQ tests tend to be standardised on a sample of the population which mainly involves people of average intellectual ability (Webb and Whitaker, 2012). This means that the tests have not been designed to accurately measure intelligence of those who make up just over 2 per cent of the population.

Further, it has been argued that class and cultural bias, which we examined in Section 2, is also an important issue. Studies carried out in different countries around the world have consistently found that among those who are classified as having special educational needs due to impaired intellectual ability, there is a disproportionate number of children from ethnic minorities or from lower socio-economic background (Leonard et al., 2003; Shifrer et al., 2010). These are precisely the groups that have traditionally been disadvantaged by IQ tests. It is therefore possible that inaccuracies of measurement identified by Whitaker (2008) combine with issues of class and cultural bias to doubly disadvantage certain already underprivileged groups in society.

3.4 Moving beyond the IQ

With the imprecision of IQ measurement and the class and cultural bias in mind, Webb and Whitaker (2012, p. 442) have concluded that the current diagnostic process is based on the 'passive acceptance of a flawed definition [of learning disability] and unreliable measurement'. This is a view shared by many psychologists, and is reflected in the official documents on the issue published by the BPS (2000). Dissenting voices have also been heard among the legal profession, including judges, who have long argued that the emphasis on an arbitrary IQ cut-off point of 70 is inappropriate when assessing the legal rights of people with learning disability, and that judgements about a person's intellectual abilities must be made on a case-by-case basis (Gudjonsson and Haward, 1998).

For these reasons, there have been a number of suggestions about how the definition of learning disability could be revised in a way that moves away from IQ measurement. Whitaker (2008, p. 8) proposed the following definition:

> A person can be regarded as having a learning disability if they are judged to be in need of community care or educational services due to a failure to cope with intellectual demands of their environment and are suffering significant distress or are unable to take care of themselves or their dependents or unable to protect themselves or their dependents against significant harm or exploitation.

Activity 3.3

Take a closer look at Whitaker's definition. As is often the case with formal definitions, a lot of information has been crammed within a single sentence. See if you can identify the key features of the proposed definition. How does it differ from the one currently in use, which you read about in Section 3.1?

The first thing to note is that there is much less emphasis on 'significant impairment of intellectual functioning'. There is an acknowledgement that someone who has a learning disability will have difficulties coping with 'intellectual demands' of their environment, but this impairment is not described in terms of a score on an IQ test. The key criterion is whether impairment of intellectual abilities prevents them from doing certain things in life. Therefore, the emphasis shifts away from the measure of IQ to a more qualitative assessment of a person's ability to live independently in a way that poses no significant risk to themselves and others, to adapt to their environment and to engage with people around them. As Webb and Whitaker (2012, p. 443) note, the central issue should not be how someone performs in a testing situation but 'whether they are able to cope, and this comes down to what society as a whole would accept as a minimum standard of quality of life'.

Summary

- Scores on IQ tests are a core criterion for assessing learning disability. A score of less than 70 is required for a learning disability diagnosis.

- The score of 70 has been selected because, following the assumption that intelligence is normally distributed, scores lower than 70 occur in only 2 per cent of the population and therefore represent an extreme score.

- IQ scores are recognised to be inexact, with a 4-point margin of error, but up to a 13-point margin of error for people who do not perform well on IQ tests. Accordingly, IQ tests may not be suitable for diagnosing learning disabilities.

- An alternative definition of learning disability has been proposed, which focuses on people's ability to cope independently.

4   Emotional intelligence

Behind the proposed revision to the definition of learning disability is the assumption that human intellectual functioning needs to be defined more broadly than the concept of IQ, and that what a person can or cannot do needs to be viewed in the appropriate context. This was also the essence of the more general critique of intelligence outlined in Section 2. There it was argued that IQ tests contain an inevitable class and cultural bias, and therefore that the singular concept of general intelligence, as measured by IQ tests, does not adequately capture the varied ways in which people reason, solve problems, and engage with complex ideas or learn from experience in everyday life.

In intelligence research, the idea that what counts as intelligence depends on context is not new. For a long time, even advocates of intelligence testing have been aware that IQ is not the only aspect of human psychological functioning that enables a person to live effectively within their environment. One of the leading figures in the history of intelligence measurement, David Wechsler, the author of the Wechsler intelligence scales, acknowledged that 'intelligent behaviour' extends beyond the kind of abilities measured by an IQ test. For Wechsler, the defining feature of intelligence was 'the capacity of the individual to act purposefully, to think rationally, and to deal effectively with [the] environment' (Wechsler, 1958, p. 3). While this involves abstract thinking, problem solving, and other abilities measured by IQ tests, it also includes things like possessing social skills.

Since the 1980s in particular, there have been some attempts to broaden the concept of intelligence, to include social skills, creative abilities and practical knowledge (Sternberg, 1985; Gardner, 1999). Gardner (1999) even proposed the idea of 'musical intelligence' – the ability to perceive and create rhythm and harmony, and 'body-kinetic intelligence' – the ability to carry out movement. And yet research on intelligence has for the most part resisted the call for the concept to be broadened, and has remained focused on the same set of abilities that has defined intelligence testing since the early twentieth century. Nevertheless, in recent decades one new type of 'intelligence' has managed to capture the imagination of both psychologists and the general public: *emotional intelligence*.

4.1   What is emotional intelligence?

The term 'emotional intelligence' was first coined in 1990 by two American psychologists, Peter Salovey and John D. Mayer. They defined it as 'a form of social intelligence that involves the ability to monitor one's own and others' feelings and emotions, to discriminate among them, and to use this information to guide one's thinking and action' (Salovey and Mayer, 1990, p. 189). They justified using the term 'intelligence' by appealing to Wechsler's definition quoted above. Intelligence, they argued, includes competence in emotional aspects of purposeful and rational behaviour.

Salovey and Mayer's work emerged at a time when it was becoming apparent that standard IQ measures were not as good at predicting job performance or educational outcome as many had believed. It appeared that other things including perseverance, empathy and the ability to control one's emotions, or get along with others, were more important (Cherniss, 2000). 'Emotional intelligence' sought to capture some of these factors within a single concept.

However, the term 'emotional intelligence' came into popular use only in the mid-1990s with the publication of the bestseller by Daniel Goleman (1995) entitled *Emotional Intelligence: Why It Can Matter More Than IQ*. Since the publication of Goleman's book, the idea of emotional intelligence has become a shorthand for the kind of social and emotional skills that are thought to bring success, and it is routinely used by politicians and the media. While some psychologists are cautious about Goleman's arguments, the popularity of emotional intelligence has left a mark on educational policy in the UK and across the world. This is important given how influential intelligence testing has traditionally been in schools. In 2007, the British government introduced a programme called Social and Emotional Aspects of Learning (SEAL), which it claimed offered a 'whole-school approach to promoting the social and emotional skills that underpin effective learning, positive behaviour, regular attendance, staff effectiveness and the emotional health and well-being of all who learn and work in schools' (DCSF, 2007, p. 4). A report published in 2010 indicated that the scheme was being implemented in 90 per cent of primary and 70 per cent of secondary schools in the UK (Humphrey et al., 2010). The SEAL programme drew extensively on the work of Goleman (1995), and effectively sought to promote the development of emotional intelligence. Similar programmes have been developed in other parts of the world too (Brackett et al., 2011).

4.2   Measuring emotional intelligence

Enshrined in the concept of emotional intelligence is the idea that, just like IQ, it can be measured. Over the years, a series of different tests of emotional intelligence have been created for use mainly in applied settings, such as the lucrative market of job recruitment and selection.

In this section, we will focus on the test which has been developed by a team of researchers led by Mayer and Salovey, the two psychologists who first suggested the term 'emotional intelligence'. The Mayer–Salovey–Caruso Emotional Intelligence Test (MSCEIT), first published in 2002, consists of 141 items and takes about 40 minutes to complete. It can be administered either as a pen-and-paper test, or by using a computer (Mayer et al., 2002).

The MSCEIT contains some important parallels with measures of IQ. First, emotional intelligence is treated as a broad ability which underpins the performance on a range of specific tasks. Second, this ability is assessed through the application of a carefully designed test which measures different components of emotional intelligence to derive an overall score. Third, just like with IQ testing, the different components are used to draw conclusions about the structure of emotional intelligence.

In Chapter 1, Figure 1.7, of *Investigating Intelligence*, you saw the structure of intelligence according to the Wechsler Adult Intelligence Scale.

Emotional intelligence is thought to consist of four components or 'branches':

- **Perceiving emotion**. This refers to how good one is at recognising emotion in oneself and others, from facial expressions, language, contextual cues, etc. This ability also involves recognising the emotional content in objects and art.

- **Using emotion**. This is the ability to harness emotions to enable things like thinking, problem solving, or communicating with others.

- **Understanding emotion**. This includes the ability to accurately label emotions and recognise the similarities and differences between various emotions and emotional responses.

- **Managing emotion**. This refers to the ability to modify one's emotions and emotional responses, and to recognise the

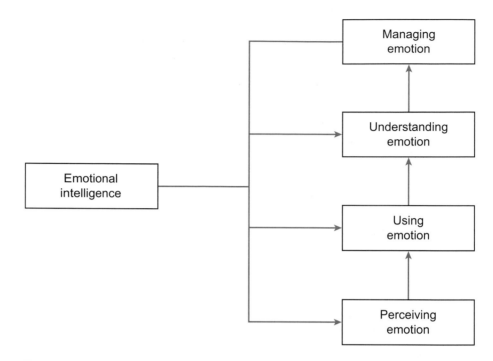

Figure 3.4   The structure of emotional intelligence according to the Mayer–Salovey–Caruso Emotional Intelligence Test

Source: adapted from Brackett et al., 2011, p. 92

appropriateness of different feelings (both one's own and those of others) in a specific context.

The diagram in Figure 3.4 shows the structure of emotional intelligence according to the authors of the MSCEIT. This structure of emotional intelligence assumes that, although separate, the four abilities are interrelated and also that they are organised in a hierarchy. The lowest branch – perceiving emotion – represents the most basic ability, while managing emotion is at the top, as the most complex of the four components of emotional intelligence. The implication here is that someone could be highly skilled at a more basic ability (e.g. recognising emotions), and not very good at the higher-level ability (e.g. determining the appropriateness of different feelings in a specific context), but not vice versa. To be good at a higher-level aspect of emotional intelligence, one needs to be competent in the lower-order processes.

In the MSCEIT, the 141 items are divided into eight different subtests, or 'tasks', two for each branch of emotional intelligence. Figure 3.5 shows four examples of the kind of items that feature on the test.

1) Debbie just came back from vacation. She was feeling peaceful and content. How well would each action preserve her mood?

Action 1: She started to make a list of things at home that she needed to do.

    very   *very*
ineffective......1..............2..............3..............4..............5......*effective*

Action 2: She began thinking about where and when she would go on her next vacation.

    very   *very*
ineffective......1..............2..............3..............4..............5......*effective*

Action 3: She decided it was best to ignore the feeling since it wouldn't last anyway.

    very   *very*
ineffective......1..............2..............3..............4..............5......*effective*

---

2) What mood(s) might be helpful to feel when meeting in-laws for the very first time?

                  not useful   *useful*

a) slight tension ....1..............2..............3..............4..............5......

b) surprise   ......1..............2..............3..............4..............5......

c) joy   ......1..............2..............3..............4..............5......

---

3) Identify the emotional expression on the picture:

    no   *extreme*
happiness......1..............2..............3..............4..............5......*happiness*

    no   *extreme*
fear......1..............2..............3..............4..............5......*fear*

---

4) Tom felt anxious, and became a bit stressed when he thought about all the work he needed to do. When his supervisor brought him an additional project, he felt _____ . (Select the best choice)

a) overwhelmed   b) depressed   c) ashamed   d) self-conscious   e) jittery

Figure 3.5   Examples of items featured in the Mayer–Salovey–Caruso Emotional Intelligence Test

Source: adapted from http://www.emotionaliq.org/

Activity 3.4

What did you think of the examples in Figure 3.5? There are two things that we would like you to consider here. First, see if you can determine which of the four 'branches' of emotional intelligence each question measures. Second, consider what you think would be the correct answer to each question. What is a helpful emotion to feel when meeting one's in-laws? How happy, or fearful, is the person in the photo? If you were designing a similar test, how would you determine what the correct answer is?

Question 1, which asks you to put yourself in Debbie's shoes, measures the ability to *manage emotions*, which includes choosing a course of action that will preserve (or get rid of) a particular feeling. Question 2 is about *using emotions* to facilitate interpersonal communication (note that you are asked what emotion would be *helpful* to feel when meeting in-laws). Question 3 measures the ability to *perceive emotion*, and to read another person's emotional expression. Question 4 assesses the ability to *understand emotion*, which is about interpreting complex feelings and appreciating the difference between labels used to describe emotions.

But what about the correct answers? The authors of the MSCEIT argue that there is, strictly speaking, no right or wrong answer to any of these questions, at least not in an absolute sense. This is where measures of emotional intelligence differ from IQ testing. With things like mental arithmetic, recalling numbers, general knowledge questions or Raven's matrices, there is a clear-cut correct answer with which a person's response can be compared. With emotional intelligence, this is not the case.

Instead, calculating someone's emotional intelligence using the MSCEIT involves what is known as *consensus scoring*: each person's responses are compared with those of thousands of people who have already taken the test and whose answers are kept in a database. So, rather than looking at whether an answer is *the* correct one, the test looks at how a person's answer compares with other people's (Brackett et al., 2011).

Consensus scoring is deemed to be appropriate because some of the main features of emotional intelligence – such as the ability to perceive, understand and manage emotions – are based on *common understanding* between people about what emotions are, what constitutes an appropriate emotional response in a situation, and so on.

As an additional check, the authors of the MSCEIT also asked a group of experts, specifically 21 members of the International Society for Research on Emotions, to indicate, based on current research on emotions, which of the answers they think would be most likely to be chosen by someone high in emotional intelligence. According to the authors of the test, the expert opinion matches the consensus-based answers very well (Brackett et al., 2011), which, the authors argue, offers reassurance that consensus scoring works and that the test is a valid measure of 'emotional intelligence' (Brackett et al., 2011).

4.3   Managing emotions: intelligence, personality or skill?

Since the MSCEIT was first developed, several studies have examined the extent to which scores on this test predict performance in the workplace. Those scoring high on an emotional intelligence test were likely to receive a positive rating from their line manager, were more likely to be satisfied with their job and cope with stress, and tended to be seen as better leaders. Results such as these have contributed to the commercial success of emotional intelligence testing, which is today used extensively in job recruitment.

The finding that managing emotions is relevant to success in the workplace is not all that surprising, however. As Goleman (2000) points out, regardless of the nature of the job, most abilities which are deemed to be essential for effective performance in the workplace refer to emotional competencies and social skills, not intellectual abilities captured by traditional IQ measures.

Yet, within the research on emotional intelligence, the central question has been not whether the concept has practical application, but rather *what it is*. Some measures, like the MSCEIT, tend to focus exclusively on emotions. Other researchers have defined the concept more broadly to include things like social skills; for example, identifying with people in the same group, solving problems between people, etc. One definition even includes 'optimism' as a feature of emotional intelligence even though it is not obviously linked to emotions (Bar-On, 2004).

Figure 3.6   Monitoring feelings and emotion: a key to success in the workplace?

There are also considerable debates about whether emotional intelligence is 'intelligence' at all. As we have seen, Salovey and Mayer (1990) defined and measured emotional intelligence as a mental *ability*, an emotional equivalent to IQ. However, other authors have suggested that it is misleading to view emotional intelligence in this way, arguing instead that controlling, managing or perceiving emotions is not so much an ability, but an aspect of **personality** (Petrides et al., 2004). Psychologists have long argued that personality characteristics such as whether someone is outgoing, assertive, perceptive or imaginative are crucially important for how a person will behave and relate to people around them. This is precisely what emotional intelligence seeks to capture.

Personality
A person's stable and enduring traits and characteristics which lead them to behave in a steady way over time. You will learn about personality in Chapter 1 of *Investigating Psychology*.

Finally, emotional intelligence is widely regarded as a *skill*, one that can be taught and developed. Programmes such as SEAL, which operates in UK schools, or the multitude of training courses and self-help books on improving emotional intelligence that have emerged in recent years, are founded on the notion that recognising, managing and controlling emotion is something that can be learned.

It is likely that debates about what emotional intelligence is – whether it is an ability, a personality characteristic or a learnable skill – will continue in the years to come. Probably the greatest value of the concept of emotional intelligence has been to emphasise the importance of social and emotional competencies for achievement in schools or in the workplace. At the same time, the lack of clarity about the precise meaning of emotional intelligence and what it comprises remains a major limitation. What is more, the very idea of emotional *intelligence* leads to the tendency to treat it as a precise and measurable 'thing' rather than as a more complex set of skills, competencies and abilities that, while playing a major role in human psychological functioning, may defy being encompassed into a single concept.

Summary

- Emotional intelligence refers to the capacity to understand and manage one's own and other people's emotions successfully.

- The concept of emotional intelligence became popular in the 1990s, and a programme promoting the teaching of emotional intelligence (SEAL) was launched in UK schools in 2007.

- The Mayer–Salovey–Caruso Emotional Intelligence Test (MSCEIT) measures four components of emotional intelligence: perceiving emotion, using emotion, understanding emotion, and managing emotion. These components are thought to be organised hierarchically, with managing emotion held to be the most complex.

- It is unclear whether what is referred to as emotional intelligence is an ability, a personality characteristic or a learnable skill.

5   Conclusion

In this final chapter, we have broadened our exploration of the psychological research on intelligence beyond its historical origins to consider alternative ways of thinking about the assessment of human intellectual abilities. We began by considering whether it is possible to devise a way of measuring or assessing intelligence that is universally applicable and without any class or cultural bias. Raven's Progressive Matrices provided an example of one test which has been heralded as such a culture-free measure. However, even there it has been argued persuasively that performance is inescapably influenced by a person's level of familiarity with the principles of sitting tests, experience with pen-and-paper puzzles, and the confidence and motivation they bring to the test. In other words, even the most basic aspect of an intelligence test – the very fact of it *being* a test – is a source of bias and one that cannot be overcome simply by making new more sophisticated versions. Consequently, as Richardson (1998, 2002) has suggested, it makes more sense to think of performance on intelligence tests as a measure of distance – near or far – from the culturally valued abilities reflected in a test. One conclusion that can be drawn from this is that rather than try to overcome culture or class bias in intelligence testing, a more useful way forward might be to try to develop ways of assessing how a person uses their mental abilities to deal effectively with their environment in real-life, everyday contexts, rather than in an artificial testing situation.

A similar conclusion was suggested in regard to the assessment of learning disability. Traditionally, IQ scores have been core to diagnosing learning disabilities despite clear evidence that the IQ score of 70, the long-standing threshold for diagnosis, is not a reliable indicator of what people can or cannot actually do. Consequently, there is a growing argument that the central issue in assessing learning disability, and the nature of the support that is best suited for particular individuals, should focus on the aspects of life that people can or cannot cope with.

The final topic in this chapter was an alternative kind of intelligence: emotional intelligence. The idea behind emotional intelligence is that understanding and managing emotions is an important ability for success, both in personal relationships and in the workplace. Like IQ, emotional intelligence is said to be measureable. However, unlike general intelligence, there is considerable debate in the literature about whether this aspect of psychological functioning is best viewed as a mental ability, a personality characteristic, or a skill that can be learned and developed.

All three topics covered in this chapter have an important feature in common. They point to the need to think about the social and cultural context in which intelligence is being defined and assessed. Definitions of intelligence, in standard IQ tests, in Raven's Progressive Matrices, in concepts such as fluid intelligence or emotional intelligence, are inescapably cultural concepts influenced by the particular abilities valued in the society in which they have emerged and in which they operate. Moreover, they point to the fact that human intellectual functioning – in other words *acting intelligently* – involves more than a small set of discrete abilities that can be measured using a psychological test. Thus, assessing intelligence ought to involve looking at a broader set of abilities and skills that enables a person to meet the intellectual and practical challenges of living in a complex world, and it should recognise that psychological functioning is deeply embedded within the broader social and cultural environment in which human beings exist.

References

Abdel-Khalek, A. M. and Raven, J. (2006) 'Normative data from the standardization of Raven's Standard Progressive Matrices in Kuwait in an international context', *Social Behaviour and Personality: An International Journal*, vol. 34, pp. 169–80.

Bar-On, R. (2004) 'The Bar-On Emotional Quotient Inventory (EQ-i): rationale, description and psychometric properties', in Geher, G. (ed.) *Measuring Emotional Intelligence: Common Ground and Controversy*, Hauppauge, NY, Nova Science.

Brackett, M. A., Rivers, S. E. and Salovey, P. (2011) 'Emotional intelligence: implications for personal, social, academic, and workplace success', *Social and Personality Psychology Compass*, vol. 5, no. 1, pp. 88–103.

British Psychological Society (BPS) (2000) *Learning Disability: Definitions and Contexts*, Leicester, British Psychological Society.

Cherniss, C. (2000) 'Emotional intelligence: what it is and why it matters', Paper presented at the Annual Meeting of the Society for Industrial and Organizational Psychology, 15 April, New Orleans, LA.

Deary, I. J. (2003) 'Ten things I hated about intelligence research', *The Psychologist*, vol. 16, no. 10, pp. 534–7.

Department for Children, Schools and Families (DCSF) (2007) *Social and Emotional Aspects of Learning for Secondary Schools*, Nottingham, DCSF Publications.

Department of Health (2001) *Valuing People: A New Strategy for Learning Disability for the 21st Century* [Online]. Available at http://www.archive.official-documents.co.uk/document/cm50/5086/5086.pdf (Accessed 19 December 2013).

Emerson, E., Hatton, C., Robertson, J., Roberts, H., Baines, S., Evison, F. and Glover, G. (2012) *People with Learning Disabilities in England 2011*, Public Health England [Online]. Available at http://www.improvinghealthandlives.org.uk/publications/1063/People_with_Learning_Disabilities_in_England_2011 (accessed 4 December 2013).

Gardner, H. (1999) *Intelligence Reframed*, New York, NY, New Books.

Goleman, D. (1995) *Emotional Intelligence: Why It Can Matter More Than IQ*, New York, NY, Bantam Books.

Goleman, D. (2000) *Working with Emotional Intelligence*, New York, NY, Bantam Books.

Gudjonsson, G. H. and Haward, L. R. C. (1998) *Forensic Psychology: A Guide to Practice*, London, Routledge.

Harkness, S., Super, C., and Keefer, C. (1992) 'Culture and ethnicity', in Levine, M. D., Carey, W. B. and Crocker, A. C. (eds) *Developmental-Behavioral Pediatrics*, 2nd edn, Philadelphia, PA, Saunders.

Humphrey, N., Lendrum, A and Wigelsworth, M. (2010) 'Social and emotional aspects of learning (SEAL) programme in secondary schools: national evaluation', UK Department of Education [Online]. Available at https://www.gov.uk/government/uploads/system/uploads/attachment_data/file/181718/DFE-RR049.pdf (Accessed 19 December 2013).

Leonard, H., Petterson, B., Bower, C. and Sanders, R. (2003) 'Prevalence of intellectual disability in Western Australia', *Paediatric and Perinatal Epidemiology*, vol. 17, pp. 58–67.

Mayer, J. D., Salovey, P. and Caruso, D. R. (2002) *Mayer-Salovey-Caruso Emotional Intelligence Test (MSCEIT)*, Toronto, Ontario, Multi-Health Systems, Inc.

Nisbett, R. E., Aronson, J., Blair, C., Dickens, W., Flynn, J., Halpern, D. F. and Turkheimer, E. (2012) 'Intelligence: new findings and theoretical developments', *American Psychologist*, vol. 67, no. 2, pp. 130–59.

Petrides, K. V., Frederickson, N. and Furnham, A. (2004) 'The role of trait emotional intelligence in academic performance and deviant behavior at school', *Personality and Individual Differences*, vol. 36, pp. 277–93.

Pinker, S. (2003) *The Blank Slate: The Modern Denial of Human Nature*, London, Penguin Books.

Raven, J., Raven, J. C. and Court, J. H. (1998) *Manual for Raven's Progressive Matrices and Vocabulary Scales, Section 1: General Overview*, San Antonio, TX, Harcourt Assessment.

Raven, J. C. (1960) *Guide to the Standard Progressive Matrices*, London, H. K. Lewis.

Richardson, K. (1998) *The Origins of Human Potential: Evolution, Development and Psychology*, London, Routledge.

Richardson, K. (2002) 'What IQ tests test', *Theory & Psychology*, vol. 12, no. 3, pp. 283–314.

Salovey, P. and Mayer, J. (1990) 'Emotional intelligence', *Imagination, Cognition, and Personality*, vol. 9, no. 3, pp. 185–211.

Shifrer, D., Muller, C. and Callahan, R. (2010) 'Disproportionality and learning disabilities: parsing apart race, socioeconomic status, and language', *Journal of Learning Disabilities*, vol. 44, no. 3, pp. 246–57.

Sternberg, R. J. (1985) *Beyond IQ: A Triarchic Theory of Human Intelligence*, New York, NY, Cambridge University Press.

Sternberg, R. J., Grigorenko, E. and Bundy, D. A. (2001) 'The predictive value of IQ', *Merrill-Palmer Quarterly*, vol. 47, pp. 1–41.

Ward, M. M. (2013) 'Parental educational attainment and sense of control in mid- and late-adulthood', *Developmental Psychology*, vol. 49, no. 7, pp. 1407–12.

Webb, J. and Whitaker, S. (2012) 'Defining learning disability', *The Psychologist*, vol. 25, no. 6, pp. 440–3.

Wechsler, D. (1958) *The Measurement and Appraisal of Adult Intelligence*, 4th edn, Baltimore, MD, The Williams & Wilkins Company.

Whitaker, S. (2004) 'Hidden learning disability', *British Journal of Learning Disabilities*, vol. 32, pp. 139–43.

Whitaker, S. (2008) 'The stability of IQ in people with low intellectual ability', *Intellectual and Developmental Disabilities*, vol. 46, pp. 120–28.

Wober, M. (1974) 'Towards an understanding of the Kiganda concept of intelligence', in Berry, J. W. and Dasen, P. R. (eds) *Culture and Cognition*, London, Methuen.

Yang, S. and Sternberg, R. J. (1997) 'Taiwanese Chinese people's conceptions of intelligence', *Intelligence*, vol. 25, pp. 21–36.

Conclusion

Well done on completing the three chapters of *Investigating Intelligence*. We hope that you enjoyed the examination of some of the themes and controversies that have defined psychological research on intelligence over the past century and a half. In this short conclusion, we will revisit the broader issues raised in the book and flag some of the themes that you will explore in more detail in the rest of the module.

An important message of *Investigating Intelligence* is that, despite more than a century of research, intelligence is still a highly contested and elusive concept. There is still little consensus on what intelligence actually is. There is also disagreement about whether there is one overarching intelligence – what Charles Spearman first referred to, more than 100 years ago, as *g* – or if it would be more productive to think of several discrete forms of intelligence, such as fluid and crystallised intelligence, or verbal and non-verbal intelligence. There are also important debates about whether the term 'intelligence' should be reserved for abilities like abstract thinking and problem solving, or whether it should be extended to incorporate things like recognising and managing emotions. There is even less agreement on how to explain differences in intelligence between people, or whether these differences are in any way relevant to people's lives. There is an important lesson in this. Psychological research seldom offers certainty or produces unanimous agreement. Human psychological functioning is immensely complex, and our understanding of it is gradually built through scientific debates, competing theories and explanations, and different ways of studying the mind and behaviour. The key thing to remember, however, is that psychology is a science, and this means that arguments must always be based on evidence, gathered through research.

You will learn more about psychology as a science in the 'General introduction' to *Investigating Psychology*.

In spite of the many disagreements and heated debates about intelligence, two things are quite clear. First, there is still a lot that we don't know about intelligence, and second, human intellectual abilities are influenced by an intricate combination of very diverse factors. These are factors to do with genes, biology and the brain, but also to do with a complex set of environmental influences such as the relationship with parents and peers, educational opportunities, class, culture, and so on. The importance of the environment is worth stressing, given how often intelligence is seen as something that we are born with, and which is fixed. As you found out from reading *Investigating Intelligence*, intelligence, whatever it may be, is deeply embedded in the broader social environment which people inhabit. How intelligence is defined and assessed, and the conditions under which people undergo IQ tests and how they perform, are inseparable from the broader cultural practices, values and assumptions about what mental abilities are worth studying and measuring. The two themes, the *interaction between nature and nurture*, and the way in which *human psychological functioning is situated in the broader social and cultural context*, run through the study of psychology. You will encounter them again and again as you continue to work through DE100 *Investigating psychology 1*, and the modules that follow.

Related to the question of multiple influences on individual psychology is another theme which permeates the pages *of Investigating Intelligence*. It is the need for an awareness that *psychological research is itself the product of the social and historical period in which it was carried out*. History and society have a profound effect on the research agenda, on the kind of questions psychologists ask, and on how they go about looking for answers. In Chapter 1, for example, you read that the origins of modern-day intelligence testing can be traced back to Alfred Binet, who was working in Paris at the time when the French government introduced a policy promoting education for all children. It was in this specific political and historical context that Binet, along with Théodore Simon, devised a system for identifying those children who needed extra help. Thus, intelligence testing of children was born. But the application of intelligence tests took a major turn with the onset of the First World War and the decision in the United States in 1917 to test all army recruits in the expectation that results could be used to allocate recruits to military roles. This military requirement brought about mass application of intelligence testing on a scale that had not been seen before. Therefore, a different social and political context – one that was characterised by the need for the more 'efficient' mass testing and where the eugenics movement guided the research agenda – generated a very different approach to intelligence, one that resulted in some of the most contentious, divisive, but also flawed, claims in the history of psychology.

The failings of the army mental testing programme illustrate the fourth key theme running throughout the chapters of this book, but also the module as a whole: the need for *critical questioning of claims to knowledge*. Do you remember from Chapter 1 the assumptions made by craniometrists, that a large head would predict a high intelligence, or by Francis Galton that physical attributes such as strength would be mirrored by psychological attributes such as intelligence? All assumptions, whether they seem sensible or foolish, should be questioned carefully. You saw another example of this in Chapter 2, Section 4.3, which discussed the assumptions made in heritability studies about the environment in which twins are raised. At first sight, the assumption that twins raised together experience roughly equal environments, or that twins raised apart necessarily grow up in different environments, seems fairly straightforward. And yet closer scrutiny of the evidence suggested that this is not so, which then gives rise to questions about some of the conclusions of heritability studies. This willingness to question the claims made by researchers and the conclusions they draw from studies is vital to any science. After all, it was the readiness to question ideas and interpretations which unearthed the incongruous and prejudiced conclusions that Robert Yerkes drew from the army mental testing programme. Today, the long-standing tradition of using IQ scores as a criterion for the diagnosis of learning disability is also being questioned, as is the claim, inherent in heritability research, that the relative importance of genes and the environment can be meaningfully separated and estimated in a fairly straightforward manner. Scientific knowledge, including our understanding of psychology, proceeds because ideas are held up to constant scrutiny, assumptions are questioned, methods are examined, evidence is cross-checked and interrogated, and the interpretations and conclusions are constantly reappraised and evaluated on the basis of new research findings. The need to critically question what we know and why we think we know it is a vital theme which will run throughout the module.

Doing this kind of critical questioning is a skilled business. Consequently, as you work through the module, you will learn much more about how to 'think critically' and evaluate psychological research. The key to achieving this is to understand the importance of research methods in psychology. Understanding *how* researchers have arrived at a particular finding, and appreciating the relative advantages and disadvantages of different methods, is central to thinking critically about research. This is one of the central themes of the module text, *Investigating Methods*.

Finally, perhaps more than anything else, a theme that has been inescapable throughout our exploration of intelligence is the way in which findings from psychology have the capacity to affect people's lives for good and, unfortunately, for bad. As you will learn throughout this module, psychology has always been driven by the need to address specific practical concerns. This applied aspect of psychology reveals its inherent relevance to everyday life. It is also one of the things that makes psychology such a fascinating topic of study.

Good luck with the rest of the module, and we hope that you will enjoy the investigation of psychology that lies ahead.

Acknowledgements

Grateful acknowledgement is made to the following sources:

Every effort has been made to contact copyright holders. If any have been inadvertently overlooked the publishers will be pleased to make the necessary arrangements at the first opportunity.

Figures

Figure 1.1: Copyright © Tim Hall/Getty Images; Figure 1.2: Copyright © SSP/Getty Images; Figure 1.6: Wechsler Adult Intelligence Scale, fourth Edition (WAIS-IV). Copyright © 2008 NCS Pearson, Inc. Reproduced with permission. All rights reserved; Figure 2.1: National Park Service, Statue of Liberty National Monument, Pub Dom, 20.6 #2, Bx 20. http://creativecommons.org/licenses/by-nc-nd/3.0/us; Figure 2.2: Archives of the History of American Psychology, The Center for the History of Psychology, The University of Akron; Figure 2.3: Image sourced from Yerkes, R.M. (1921) 'Psychological examining in the United States Army', *Memoirs of the National Academy of Sciences*, vol. 15, parts 1–3, Washington, D. C., Government Printing Office, p. 91. This image is in the public domain; Figure 2.4: Adapted from Yerkes, R.M. (1921) 'Psychological examining in the United States Army', *Memoirs of the National Academy of Sciences*, vol. 15, parts 1–3, Washington, D. C., Government Printing Office; Figure 2.5: Copyright © Adrian Sherratt/Alamy; Figure 2.9: Copyright © Jack Sparticus/ Alamy; Figure 3.2 left: Copyright © iStockPhoto.com/ monkeybusinessimages; Figure 3.2 top right: Copyright © Shutterstock/ Len44ik; Figure 3.2 bottom right: Copyright © Shutterstock/Richard Clarke; Figure 3.5: Copyright © iStockPhoto.com/SensorSpot; Figure 3.6: Copyright © Shutterstock/Golden Pixels LLC.

Tables

Table 2.2: Adapted from Yerkes, R.M. (1921) 'Psychological examining in the United States Army', *Memoirs of the National Academy of Sciences*, vol. 15, parts 1–3, Washington, D. C., Government Printing Office.

Index